C000185573

CLASSIC
MOUNTAIN BIKE RIDES
IN BRITAIN

TIM WOODCOCK

Dedication

For Kay, my mother, my father and my family

First published in 1995 by

Future Books

a division of Future Publishing Limited
Beauford Court, 30 Monmouth Street, Bath BA1 2BW

Text and photographs copyright © Tim Woodcock 1995

The moral right of the author has been asserted

Typeset and designed by Visual Image, Street, Somerset

Cover design by Maria Bowers

All rights reserved. No part of this work may be reproduced or utilised in any
form or by any means electronic or mechanical, including photocopying,
recording or by any information storage and retrieval system now known or
hereafter invented, without the prior permission of the publisher.

A CIP catalogue record for this book is available from the British Library

ISBN: 1 85981 016 0

Printed and bound in Singapore by Times Offset (M) Ltd. SDN BHD Group

2 4 6 8 10 9 7 5 3 1

If you would like more information on our other cycling titles please write to:
The Publisher, Future Books at the above address

Although every care has been taken by the Author in the preparation of this
book, no warranty is given by either the Author or the Publisher as to the
accuracy or completeness of the information contained within it, and neither
the Author nor the Publisher shall be responsible or liable for any loss or
damage whatsoever arising by virtue of such information or any instructions or
advice contained within this book or by use of the aforementioned.

CLASSIC
MOUNTAIN BIKE RIDES
IN BRITAIN

TIM WOODCOCK

future
BOOKS

Contents

Foreword

The beauty and variety of our countryside has a strong hold on the British soul. The land has been formed by, and formed, the people of this Island for countless centuries and there is no nation more romantically attached to the landscapes which produce such an instant sense of place. Our place.

It happens for me going west off the flat from Salisbury, as the hills rise around me and the horizon closes in. Huddling in more and more closely, until, completely surrounded by the tors of Dartmoor, I know I am home.

Generations of British people have found their greatest rest, inspiration and sense of belonging in our mountains, moors, hills and valleys. No, we don't talk about it much, but we vote with our feet. Or, these days, with our tyres, as the mountain bike takes us as far into the wilds of an afternoon as a weekend of walking.

To enjoy unspoilt countryside in peaceful solitude today, one has to go a lot further from civilisation than ever before and there's so little time. The ability of the mountain bike to take us deep into the country with no more noise or erosion than if we were walking, has a great deal to do with its popularity.

But the British countryside is challenging as well as beautiful. Taking on those longer routes, no matter how fit one is, requires a good deal of skill and knowledge. The best way to accrue that knowledge is to ride some well tried and classic routes in the company of an experienced friend.

Someone like Tim Woodcock, the author of this book. Tim is not only an enthusiastic and experienced long-distance trail rider, he has a painter's eye for the British landscape, which expresses itself in the sometimes achingly beautiful photographs, the result, often, of hours waiting until the light is exactly right.

If you can't take Tim, then this book is an excellent substitute. In fact it's hardly a substitute at all - he has a way of making you feel he's with you every step of the way.

Tym Manley

AUTHOR'S NOTE

Split into nine regions within England, Scotland and Wales and featuring more than 40 day rides, this is an extraordinary ride guide. It is a distillation of only the very best routes published in *MTB Pro* magazine's Pro Trails – and then some. All of them have been planned with local mountain bikers and then ridden by the Pro Trails team. That wealth of local trail knowledge ensures that wherever you decide to take your wheels and test your trail skills you're going to experience the very best off-road routes around.

This book is a celebration of mountain biking in Britain – in words, pictures and routes. In essence what lies between these covers is the inspiration to get out there, play the trail, focus on the intimate encounter between tyre and terrain and immerse yourself in the landscape. Read, enjoy, then ride!

Tim Woodcock

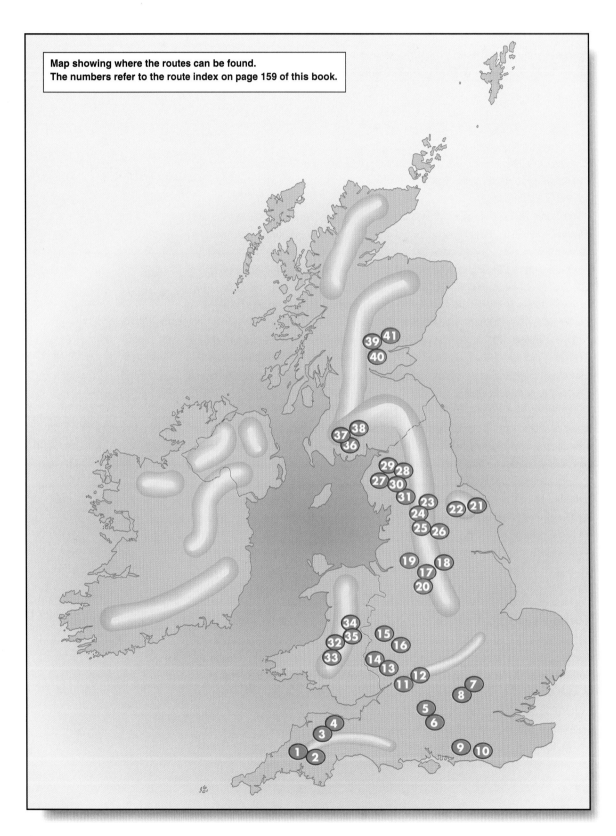

Map showing where the routes can be found.
The numbers refer to the route index on page 159 of this book.

Introduction

HOW TO USE THE ROUTE GUIDES

PLANNING YOUR DAY

Routes

The routes described in this book have been designed as one-day circular tours for off-road cyclists with at least a basic level of competence in mountain biking. Of necessity 'day' is a very broad generalisation as the time of year, weather, ground conditions and the riders' abilities will determine actual ride-time.

Times

The time given for each route is based on the assumption that the riders are fit, experienced and the stops are few and far between. For the rest of us a good starting point is to allow an average speed of about 3–4mph in winter and 5–6mph in summer, with a penalty of 1–2mph if the weather or ground conditions are bad. By habitually taking note of your estimated performance by comparison with your actual ride–time, you will soon get a good idea of how long your real 'day ride' can be.

Distance and height gain

Rides of 20 miles or less can usually be slotted into a day with ease, but rides of 30 miles and more need more careful scheduling. Although the length of each ride is an important factor, don't be a slave to mileage. For the mountain biker height gain is probably the most important, single determinant in the effort expended during a ride. As a rule of thumb, rides making more than an average climb rate of 1000ft/10 miles will be strenuous – you need to be fit to really enjoy

them! A day with more than 3500ft of height gain is going to be tough, especially in winter when daylight hours are few.

Grades

Each route has been given a grading according to its combined technical and physical demands:

A Low/moderate technical demands; not too strenuous.

B Moderate technical demands; some hard cycling involved.

C Moderate/difficult technical sections; strenuous riding

D Difficult/severe technical route; physically very tough.

These grades are subjective and are relevant only to the routes in this book.

Maps

This guide book is armchair inspiration and it's not designed to be used on the trail. Consequently the maps have been drawn to enable you to transfer the information to the relevant Ordnance Survey map specified in the information section accompanying each route. OS Outdoor Leisure 1:25 000 scale maps covering many of the routes are available laminated and these are recommended for use on the trail – they are much easier to handle when it's windy. Otherwise you can laminate paper maps between two sheets of waterproof 'transpa-seal' or you can carry spray-proofed maps in plastic bags; A5-size clear plastic, zipped document cases are ideal. Always carry the map folded to show the terrain you are crossing, as this will help you gauge the route ahead.

CHAPTER ONE

Before you Go

Travel light and ride free. Whatever you take you've got to carry. When you're expecting to tackle some serious hills or you reckon on putting down a mega-mileage, you'll appreciate that trimming kit to a necessary minimum makes sense – especially on that last granny-cog slog before home. Providing you don't overdo it and skimp on essentials, saving weight is safer too. It conserves energy and makes handling the bike on some of the more extreme terrain a lot less hairy.

HARDWARE

If you're tempted to tackle steep and technical trails that characterise our more rugged regions then use a good-quality, reasonably light, proper MTB – 21 or more indexed gears and alloy wheels. We're talking several hundred pounds here, but if you're serious about mountain biking it's worth it. Take a look at the mountain biking press for what's what, then ask at a good mountain bike shop and buy the best that you can afford. If that's out of your budget then consider hiring one until the off-road bug has you hooked. There are bike-hire outlets in many of our National Parks and many bike shops also hire. Details are given with the relevant route guides.

TOOLS AND SPARES

Quality doesn't come cheap but good tools are a godsend when you're in a fix, so be prepared to pay for them. Most multi-tools will save weight on a tool-roll of separate bits, but don't forget to check that your clever widget does all the whatsits on your bike. The same goes for spares. It's surprising how many folk carry a spare inner tube with the wrong valve type! Once you've got all your tools and spares together, pack them tight and keep them handy – ready for the inevitable trail-side emergency.

SOFTWARE

We're all aware of the weather's potent effect on our well-being – in the wet it's doom and gloom but once the sun pops out life's a party. Clothing, like the weather, has a profound import on our level of enjoyment outdoors. Except clothing choice is not dictated on a whim of Nature. Kit yourself out with inappropriate gear that's been moth-balled in the wardrobe for the past five years and you're dressing up for a dose of doom and gloom. Uncomfortable. But take some time in selecting good-quality kit and you'll be pleased to party in the worst weather.

Even in summer, controlling warmth is the vital element, versatility the name of the game. Up on the moors and mountains the increased height and exposure to wind chill can make things unexpectedly wintry. I've been shivering in the icy blast of a savage hailstorm on High Street – in the Lake District, not in town – whilst holiday-makers down in Patterdale are bathing along the sun-warmed shores of Ullswater. If you're expecting cold, wet weather then you'll need extra clothing, especially thermals (tights, tops and socks), full gloves, headband/snood and waterproof socks. In winter a fleece/windproof top, for when you're caught in the open with an emergency repair, lined mitts and lined hood may be necessary.

INFO: HARDWARE

TOOL KIT
Pump
Tyre levers
Full set of Allen keys
Small adjustable wrench
Screwdriver (cross-head and flat)
Chain-splitter
Spoke key
Penknife

BIKE SPARES
Inner tube
Puncture repair kit
Brake blocks
Rear light/batteries
Cable ties

Kitting out a mountain biker has proved to be the outdoor clothes designers' biggest challenge yet. It's a strenuous sport, generates loads of heat at peak activity, then the loonies stand about mending punctures on a hillside with a wind-chill factor of -10°C and their body temperature drops like the proverbial stone. But designers are rising to the challenge and there's a stack of really good, MTB-specific gear to choose from.

The multi-layer principle is bandied about as the way to go – and it works – but there's always someone who has to swim against the tide. Now there are one or two manufacturers producing single-layer, pile-lined kit but it's really late season/winter wear. So right from the start we're faced with a bewildering choice of kit, complicated by contrasting design convictions and all so technical that you need a science degree to discern what's what.

The best approach is to decide what you want the clothing to do. For day-long trips it has to be light, have low bulk, be quick drying, fit well and feel comfortable. Otherwise you won't wear it! Whether it's to wick, provide warmth, windproofing or water resistance (you'll need clothing to perform all of these functions), it must perform well too. Above all it has to let your body lose moisture and 'breathe'. Under-layer clothing that soaks up water, sags like a wet flannel and dims the lights when the tumble drier's turned on is useless. Likewise, a top layer that's built like a tent, flies like a kite and gives you your very own greenhouse effect is best left at home and used as a bin-liner. MTB magazines regularly review cycling kit, back issues are easily obtainable and their advice should at least put you on the right track.

ON YOUR FEET

On your feet there's nothing to beat a good pair of MTB boots. That's boots, not shoes. But there are alternatives, such as light walking boots and even fell-running shoes with modified soles. Both grip well and give ankle support. Don't be tempted by making do with trainers unless you're good at grass skiing with a bike on your back. Even a modest grass bank can become insurmountable if your boots sport an inadequate sole.

If you have SPDs check that your shoes have a deep, aggressive tread that'll give a firm footing when it comes to shouldering the frameset. Especially over grass. Some SPDs also suffer from clogging when it gets really gloopy. And it can get seriously gloopy on the chalk downland of southern England.

Last, but definitely not least, wear a helmet!

NAVIGATION

For the most part you'll be better off with 1:25 000 scale maps such as the Outdoor Leisure, Pathfinder or Explorer series of OS maps. 1:50 000 and 1inch:1mile maps do not show the same sort of detail – field boundaries, single track etc – but are fine if you're careful to follow the route directions given. You should also have a good-quality compass on a neck cord and a weather-proof cycle computer – both of which you must be able to use with ease – and that's the pilot part sorted.

HEALTH SURVIVAL GEAR

Mountain biking can be dangerous; a trivial accident on a mountainside can quickly bring you down to a survival situation. A matter of life or death. Given the right kit, make the right decisions and you can turn crisis to drama, live to tell the tale and even laugh about it. Later. A good first aid kit and the knowledge to use it are essential. A basic kit should include antiseptic wipes, plasters, cohesive tape for wounds, triangular bandage, salt tablets for cramp and first aid instructions. You might very well be an accomplished first-aider. Whoever comes to your aid might not and they, not to mention you, will appreciate a set of instructions ready to hand. Survival gear – mini-torch, survival bag and whistle – can all be packed with the first aid kit. Pack it in a heavy-duty, zip-tie polythene bag, label it clearly and know where it is.

BAG IT

Fell walkers are a common sight on the trail – popular walking and biking routes regularly coincide – and many of them will be strolling along with pint-sized day-packs to take their kit. Take a leaf out of their book. Travel light and leave it on your back. Either in a bum-bag or, on more adventurous winter outings, in a small rucksack – about 20litre capacity.

OFF-ROAD RIDING

Ride safe. Be light on the landscape. Being the new boys on the block, mountain bikers have run the gauntlet of being alienated by other countryside users since the word go. The sport has mushroomed and our wilderness areas have witnessed a wheeled invasion – ramblers see us as rivals, environmentalists call us erosionists, farmers fear speeding bikes will frighten stock and uncaring cyclists will flatten crops. But we are here to stay and entrenched attitudes are already changing, this will happen more quickly if we ride responsibly.

RIGHTS OF WAY

Although we've taken every care to try and ensure that the routes described in this book will keep your cycling within the law, at the very least the status of some sections will change. Plus, of course, you may get lost so it is as well to be sure of your rights of way.

Off-road cycling is permitted on bridleways, roads used as public paths (RUPPs), byways open to all traffic (BOATs), unclassified county roads (Greenways) and designated cycle paths. Some of the North West Water Authority sections of the route are open to us with the landowner's consent, and this permissive access may be revoked at any time. Cycling is not permitted on footpaths, open land or on pavements. Do not rely on signposts as reliable indicators of a route's status – local authorities do not always make correct use of bridleway (blue) and footpath (yellow) waymarkers. If in doubt, dismount. And remember, all land is owned by someone – even the remote moorland areas on this route – and you must take care not to trespass. If a landowner asks that you leave, it is in your best interests, no matter what the right and wrong of it may be, to acquiesce.

Of course, you may be bowling along a bridleway when up pops a barbed wire fence and the way is barred. It's a tricky situation because your rights are wrapped in a woolly bit of rhetoric which says you can remove the obstacle sufficiently to get past if it is reasonably possible, or make a short detour to get round it. The landowner can demand recompense if you cause any damage so clambering over it – often the instinctive reaction – is not a clever thing to do. This doesn't happen often but rights of way across farmland do get blocked, ploughed up, are over-planted or are stocked with dangerous animals. Farmers are supposed to provide signed, alternative routes, but if you're in doubt don't traipse across regardless. Check with the owner and if you're still forced off the right of way, report it to the local authority who will take up the matter on your behalf.

CODES OF CONDUCT

You won't be the first to ride these routes so you will be treading in the tyre tracks of others. If they've careered along, forged furrows across fields, stampeded livestock, left gates gaping and created a trail of havoc and mayhem, then you're not going to get a warm reception from the countryside community. Nor is anybody else who follows along unless you follow the Country and Off-Road Codes.

They're not really a set of rules so much as guidances that any responsible, thoughtful member of the mountain biking community would adopt without a second's thought.

RIDE SAFETY

Three's company, not two, and four's fine outdoors in the wilds. In the event of one getting badly injured, someone can go for help and someone can stay with the casualty. But ideally two should go for help, not one, which is why four is better. More and mountain bikers in a bunch can be an intimidating party on a narrow path.

Ability, strength and stamina in any group will vary. Keep within the capacity of everyone, watch your pace and make sure everyone keeps within sight and sound of each other. But don't bunch up, especially on downhills, or there'll be some rear-end wipe-outs. And they can be real nasty! It's always a good idea to wait for stragglers at the top of climbs, at the bottom of tricky descents and at gates. It's in the nature of a strung-out group to separate even further at such points so make sure that the young eager pup out in front is aware of it.

One of the first signs of fatigue is when your normally ebullient companion rides quiet and persistently lags behind. Don't push it. Rest, drink, eat and keep warm – exposure may be just around the corner.

Prevention is better than cure. Eat heartily a few hours before you set out and eat lots of carbohydrates. If you expect to be riding for more than a couple of hours, then make full use of the various sports recovery drinks and carbo-loading preparations now available – after all you're just as deserving of their benefits as the athletes who advertise the stuff. Try not to ride for more than one hour without having some food – not as easy as it sounds – and drink regularly and drink plenty, before you get thirsty. Don't be over-confident when assessing how much trail should pass under your tyres during the day. Take into account the amount of height to be climbed – it's more important than mileage! The times given with each route are a guide and do not allow for stops. Even the terminally-fit will find that 40 miles or about 4000ft of height gain are about as much as they can do in one day.

INFO: COUNTRY CODE

Enjoy the countryside and respect its life
and work.
Guard against all risk of fire.
Fasten all gates.
Keep dogs under control.
Keep to public rights of way across
farmland.
Use gates and stiles to cross boundaries.
Leave livestock, crops and machinery alone.
Take your litter home.
Do not contaminate water.
Protect wild flora and fauna.
Take special care on country roads.
Make no unnecessary noise.
Cycle only on permitted rights of way.
Give way to horse riders and walkers.
Do not ride in such a manner that you are a
danger to others.
Do not race.
Keep erosion to a minimum and do not skid.
Be courteous and considerate to others.
Be self-sufficient and make sure your bike is
safe to ride.
Wear a helmet.
Follow a route marked on a map.
Follow the Country Code.

WEATHER

Out in the wilds, weather will make or break a ride. It's all in a day's mountain weather to experience sun, sleet, rain, wind, warmth, cold and calm. Maybe our highlands are minor mounds on the world map, but it can be as bleak as Arctic tundra up on the Pennines when winter gets a grip. Bleaklow, just 15 miles from Manchester's city centre, is as it sounds! It's easy to be lulled into a false sense of security, set out ill-informed and unprepared and end up the subject of a fell rescue operation. Get the most recent weather forecast from regional radio and TV channels. They give a useful overview of what's coming.

Three factors that strangers to the high moors often fail to take into account are altitude, wind and winter. As you climb, temperature falls. Roughly speaking temperature falls 1°C for every 100m gain in height (3°C per 1000ft) on a clear day; half that fall on a cloudy one. Wind-chill increases with wind strength. In a gentle to moderate breeze (force 3, about 10mph) wind-chill is about -5°C, about -10°C in a fresh, gusty breeze (force 5, about 20mph) and -15°C in a really strong wind (force 7, about 30mph).

It would be foolish to venture out onto our moors and mountains if gale-force winds are forecast, knowing that they'll be more ferocious on the higher fells. Take a furlough and live to bike another day. And be prepared to take an unplanned detour if the weather deteriorates badly whilst you're out.

LOSING YOUR WAY

Navigation can be tricky. Keeping on course depends on you, and preferably your companions as well, knowing your position at ALL times. Danger zones are forests, open moor and in poor visibility, so take care to read the terrain correctly in these situations and make no assumptions about this or that trail being a 'main' route. One way of coping with poor visibility is to follow a compass bearing to the most distant visible marker (Not a sheep because it might walk off!), cycle to it, take another bearing on the next marker, cycle and so on. Most of the routes described take you along obvious tracks, so you are more likely to feel lost than really be lost.

But, despite our best endeavours to keep you on track, there's always a chance you might wander from the route. Nobody intends to get lost and it comes as a shock. Don't panic. Stop. Regroup. Make sure everybody's with you, then stays put and only then try to work out where you went wrong. Not too far back you'll have been sure of your position. Find it on the map.

Naturally you'll have been using your cycle computer to keep a log of point-to-point distances and it's a simple matter of reading the distance off, calculating direction and that'll give you an approximate position. Forgotten to zero the trip distance at the last known point? Then estimate how long ago you were there and in which direction you have travelled during the elapsed time. Allowing for ground conditions, calculate how far you've cycled. Now check your surroundings and see if local landmarks coincide with your findings. If you're still unsure and visibility is poor then stay put until conditions improve.

In an ideal world three distinct landmarks should be recognised for you to be absolutely certain of your locality though, given two, you can still take compass bearings to position yourself. It goes without saying that correct use of the compass and trusting it, not your instincts, are vital.

FITNESS

Off-road riding is characterised by bouts of extreme effort coupled with a modicum of technical proficiency – that's jargonese for a touch of two-wheeled wizardry and trail wisdom. Often it's just your sheer determination plus a degree of dexterity with power delivery that will get you through tricky bits of trail. Either way, it all takes fitness.

But being fit is not just a question of power. It's more about recovery rate and, in mountainous terrain, legs that are quick to revive are not just an asset but a necessity. Being in shape to take a mountain bike off-road in some of our more extreme regions such as the Peak District, the Lakes, Scotland, Wales and the West Country takes time to develop but it's worth it. Fitness facilitates enjoyment. MTBers who get out and hit the hills regularly will reap the benefits – namely a quantum leap in the fun factor!

COMPANIONS

Off-roading is an enriched experience if you're in good company. A well-integrated group is much better able to overcome adversities with ease; even if it's a simple thing like bad weather. Bad weather? Yes. Biking with the elements as an adversary can be a rewarding experience, but there's always the time when you're caught out in the open and the weather closes in unexpectedly. It goes without saying that you should all get on, but don't forget fitness. One mismatch – couch potato or fitness freak – in an otherwise well-balanced band of bikers, will often lead to persistent friction and cast a shadow over a day out trail-shredding. Choose your trailmates carefully, and you will appreciate both the company and moral support, especially on the steep ascents!

CHAPTER TWO

West Country Moors

THE SOUTH WEST

Way down in the south-west corner of Britain lie hidden some of the richest off-road riding experiences these islands have to offer. Surprising, perhaps, in counties pleasant to recall as a patchwork of emerald pastures and encircled by a glittering coastline, considered by many to be the most beautiful in the world. But that gentle, sylvan scenery is rudely interrupted by the remote mass of Devon's Dartmoor National Park, that soars some 2000ft above a sea of rolling hills; and by Somerset's Exmoor National Park, where a rough 'n' tumble terrain pitches into the sea in a setting that the locals call 'Little Switzerland'. It's England's greatest off-road secret.

Dartmoor, dark and forbidding, is starkly different from its surrounding countryside. A dramatic moorland plateau, littered with granite outcrops, cut by ravines and beset by quaking bogs, it has its own bleak climate. Swirling mists, an awesome rainfall and high winds can make it a fearsome place. For the biker, Dartmoor's twisting, technical trails, together with fast forest fire-road and the dark, peat paths of the open moor, combine to create a playground of pure off-road delight, where the horizons are distant, the possibilities endless.

Exmoor is an area of recently tamed upland straddling Somerset's and Devon's northern coastlines. First time visitors are often surprised that the bleak grassland and distant horizons of their imagining come reduced to a more intimate scale. Small as Exmoor is, it boasts such a variety of contrasts – dizzy cliffs, desolate moor, sheltered valleys, bleak farmsteads, cosy hamlets, babbling brooks – that every rider leaves with a pot-pourri of lasting impressions. Cumbrian tracks, Shropshire bridleways,

D I R E C T I O N S → → → → →

Start Princetown's High Moors Centre (GR590735) Two Bridges (GR608750) and turn L (NE) for 0.15m on B3212 towards Two Bridges and Mortenhampstead. Then turn R (E) onto waymarked

bridleway 0.5m to Bachelor's Hall. R (S) to T-junction. L (ENE) up to Y-junction. Fork L (E) on track then single track for 2m to field gate on L (muddy puddle here).

Go SO (NE) through gate on posted bridleway 0.4m to field wall. SO (ENE) 400yds across pasture to join track (E) down through Sherberton Farm for 0.4m to just before bridge. Turn L (N) through gate for 0.4m on bridleway over step-stones, then alongside Swincombe River to West Dart River crossing.

SO step-stones, keep L by river for 0.4m. Swing R (NNE) for 0.4m up bridleway to B3357. Turn L over cattle grid then R (NNE) for 0.5m to turn L (NW) on unmarked, faint bridleway for 0.75m over moor to bridle-gate. Swing R (N) above forest for 0.3m then turn R (E) 100yds down tricky descent to track.

Turn L then immediately R (NE then NNW) for 1.5m forest ride, over cattle grid to B3212. Turn R (NE) 0.2m to Lydgate bridleway then

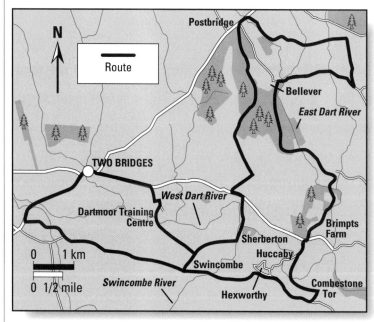

Pembrokeshire cliff-tops, Peak moorland, Yorkshire dales, Border forests – all in miniature, crammed into 300-odd square miles. It's the epitome of English off-roading at its best.

PRINCETOWN/POSTBRIDGE LOOPS

Distance: 25 miles. Time: 4.5 hours (dry), 5.5 hours (wet).

A real taste of the best that Dartmoor can deliver, embraced in a double loop. Best ridden in summer, as river crossings are dangerous after heavy rain and peat paths suffer when they're soaked.

I'd misspent a good proportion of my youth bog-trotting on Dartmoor but departed its wilderness ways for the Smoke. Now the prodigal biker had returned; a new map, old bike and keen to see how Dartmoor fared from a fat tyre point of view. It was a revelation!

Big bros Pete – we'd trodden these trails together – voiced similar thoughts as we kitted up in Postbridge car park.

turn R (SE), pass below hotel on waymarked bridleway, for 1.5m to Pizwell. Go SO (E) for 0.5m, between houses then crossing ford, on track to gate.

Turn R (S) through gate 0.4m then switch 10yds L to second trail. SO (S) 0.4m to corner field gate. Turn R (NW) 1.5m on lane. L (S) into Bellever Forest 0.25m to bridle-gate.

SO (S) for 0.75m, keeping R at Y-junction, SO at T-junction, through gate, past Laughter Hole Farm, through gate to waymarked single track opposite. Go SO (SSE then turn ENE) 0.5m to East Dart step-stones.

SO, through gate, to swing R (ESE) up single track to gate 0.5m away. Now on track go SO (SE) for 0.4m past farm to road. Turn L (E) 160yds then turn R (WSW) for

0.12m, over stream then keep R down to brook, following bank to hidden clapper bridge.

SO then L (S) by bank to East Dart step-stones. SO then L (SE) 0.75m on single track alongside river at first, then track to Brimpts Farm. Swing R around NE side of buildings. Follow drive 0.4m (WSW), SO X-roads onto track to B3357.

Turn R (W) for 140yds then turn L (S) towards Hexworthy for 0.2m. Turn hard L (SE) up bridleway for 0.1m to swing R (SSW) to gate. Go SO (SSW) 0.5m on track to West Dart step-stones.

Cross SO (SSE) for 100yds to cross two streams to gate. Go through. Fork R (SE) on mapped but undefined bridleway for 0.25m. (Trodden route is SSE for 0.2m then swing L, ESE then ENE, on obvious

single track for 0.12m to rejoin mapped bridleway.) Obvious single track climbs (ENE) for 0.2m up to track.

Turn R (S) 0.12m to lane then turn R (W) for 1m to fork L (W) at Y-junction. Continue (W) 0.25m then turn L (SW) onto bridleway for 0.75m, going SO lane and bridge, to swing L (W) by Swincombe Farm for 0.25m to gate. Go SO (WNW) for 0.2m then turn R (NNE) at bridleway X-roads for 50yds to familiar gate.

Go SO (NE) for 0.2m to turn L (NW) at waymarked bridleway junction for 1m, going SO (NW) at T-junction, over bridge, to Dartmoor Training Centre. Continue for 0.6m, turn R (NNW) at T-junction, to B3357. Turn L (WNW) for 3m, forking L (SSW) after Two Bridges, to Princetown's High Moor Centre.

I was champing at the bit. It was a magnificent May morning, the tyres hadn't shredded dirt for over a week and I was impatient to explore the moor anew. Soon enough we were kicking up dust clouds on Bellever's forest trails. An ideal warm-up and we're free to roam on all the tracks. Forestry Commission take a big vote of thanks!

Down through Laughter Hole – its fields awash with bluebells, bright against a rusty backdrop of bracken – then we diverted onto a divine piece of single track. Strategically placed granite boulders add a technical edge to the trail. Then it gets twisty, slots in a surprise trio of steps, a footbridge and finally a set of step-stones down by the Dart.

With rigs shouldered we tripped lightly over the boulders, scaled the valley side to be rewarded by yet more downhill delights. Flat at first, the drop down to Babeny develops into a demanding descent with big air-time for tricksters and a bone-jarring run-out to the road. Ten yards of tarmac – satin to shocked senses – before we dipped right, crossed a grassy sward down to an ancient, moss-covered clapper bridge. A crude scaffold of massive granite slabs. Dancing light, bluebell-bedecked woodland floor and a babbling brook conspired to distract attention from the tricky trail down the East Dart Valley.

With spring in our tail we honked up the track to Brimpts Farm, crossed their ocean of alloy-rotting ooze – oh, my Mavics! – and returned to tarmac on Huccaby Hill, high above the West Dart. A dash down the road and, right by Huccaby Farm, we hung a hair-

INFO: DARTMOOR

ACCESS

The B3212 Exeter (A30) to Yelverton (A386) road gives excellent access to central Dartmoor. The nearest mainline BR station to our routes is Plymouth (Tel: 01752 221300) about 18 miles away. The Plym Valley Cycleway facilitates off-road access to the moors and starts at Laira Bridge (over the River Plym) on the A379 Kingsbridge road and ends close to Burrator.

MAPS

OS 1:25 000 Outdoor Leisure 28 Dartmoor; OS 1:50 000 Landrangers 191 and 202.

Taking ten on Swincombe's rustic bridge

pin left, and climbed to meet muddy track. A short struggle with gloop and again Dartmoor came up trumps with a tasty single track descent. After the top step it's a breeze, with random rocks to keep your riding skills sharp until you hit the sandy shore of the West Dart. A set of flat-topped stones spanned the river. We lunched on the far side, sat in warm sun, before crossing a foot-bridge and getting completely bogged down trying to follow the map-marked bridleway. A quick back-pedal and our tracking skills ferreted out a trail of tell-tale hoof marks to follow. Circumnavigating south of the swamp, they led us to a tricky little climb – a delight if you do it without a dab – up to a cart track. We struck out south, took up on the lane over Combestone Tor where it plummets down to Saddle Bridge (a great bit of gravity suck, for road!) and along the valley side towards Sherberton Farm.

Before long we were back to bridleway, this time on track for Swincombe. With long views ahead, no knobbly bits and gradual gradient increase we swept down to Swincombe, eyes streaming in the cool air. A slabbed ramp up to the bridge nearly grabbed my wheel; Pete wisely walked over. Up to the farm, now abandoned, we shared our route with a stream then turned off into a real gnarly number. Clitter (granite rubble) carpets the track, and there's the odd step; add to that a slight incline and you've got a challenge to rise to.

Beyond the old meadows we met peat moor. Black as night in the pale grass and more slippery than axle grease, it's best ridden dry or frozen. Today it was wet, so we skipped the peat path to Princetown and did a dog-leg re-route to Prince Hall instead. A blessing in disguise as it added in a trio of top-cog downhills and a touch of technical trail down by Rue Lake river crossing. Great stuff!

Up on the B road, with time running against us, we reluctantly turned east for Bellever. We cruised across the open moor, got a speed buzz down a couple of deep little valleys and rejoined the off-road route at Dunna Bridge. I'd switched to 'That wraps it up' mode but Dartmoor still had more delights in store.

We decided on a last detour to Bellever Tor, on a bridleway that heads across Laughter Tor. That turned out to be a joke. There was no bridleway where that old bridleway should be. Just virgin heath. Pete had spotted a well-hoofed, but unmarked bridle route by the last gate. We backtracked to adopt the unofficial alternative.

Our unease at being 'illegal' was shelved once map and unofficial bridlepaths coincided on Bellever Tor's eastern flank. We zipped along the narrow path, dipped right into the forest and plummeted down a rugged chute of shattered rock. Tricky! (Keep right at the bottom unless you fancy a slow-speed drop-off.)

INFO: DARTMOOR

ACCOMMODATION

Princetown, a small community dominated by the grey fortress of HM Dartmoor Prison, has everything from a bunk barn to hotels. Two Bridges (3m NE) has a hotel and at Postbridge (10m NE) there's a camping barn, B&Bs, hotels and down in nearby Bellever a YHA (Tel: 01822 88227). More info is available from the Dartmoor National Park (Tel: 0626 832093).

Dartmoor's High Moor Centre in Princetown (Tel: 01822 890414) opens all year. It's well worth a visit if only because they sell maps, have the latest information on cycle routes and they can put visitors in touch with tourist facilities.

Hound Tor, where the Devil hangs his hat

We paused for breath at the bottom. That one took us both by surprise. Most un-Devon like! With Bellever's forest track under our tyres we spun the cranks, kicked up the pace and sped between the pines. A short climb strung us out – I still had some spring in my Smokes – then it was a final downhill fling. A touch of 40mph on a free trail was a fitting finale!

BURRATOR TOUR

Distance: 16 miles (12-mile circuit from a Burrator start).
Time: 2.5 hours (dry), 3.5 hours (wet).

A more all-weather route than the above, this is a trip round the steel-grey waters of Burrator set below Sheep Tor's rugged mount, with a 2-mile downhill to savour.

'Blustery south-easterly winds, strong to gale force over the moors, will give the low temperatures an exceptionally raw edge today...' The local forecast promised a big freeze. Bitterly cold it was, but it was the power of that incessant, tempestuous polar blast that dominated our day.

My companions for today were not keen. Dave donned every bit of fleece and Pertex he could lay his hands on, Pete asked repeatedly 'Have we got the cocoa?' and Luke, short of a head-band, was going to ride with a plastic bag over his head. Not a good idea! It might seem more pleasant than facing that Arctic air bare-browed but the side effects can be lethal! He opted for a tea towel bandanna instead.

My enthusiasm for the fray could have had an artificial boost – it was maiden mud-plugging time for my Trek Carbon Composite – and it was I who took off up the track for South Hessary Tor, hopping drainage ditches, oblivious to the buffeting head wind. A less-than-enthusiastic trio followed on. Despite the icy blast, we'd soon warmed to the trail trials that this well-used piece of path put our way. Nothing truly technical but sufficient to whet the appetite for rougher stuff. That was to come soon enough.

Beyond the grey granite slabs of the Tor a boundary stone – one of many – stood sentinel at a moorland X-roads. Here – after a brief chat to a father and son duo, daft enough to be out here too – we swung right, I hit the cranks hard and grabbed the lead on the day's opening downhill dash. Rutted and rock-strewn, the trail reverberated through stiff forks, blurring vision and kicking the bike skywards at the least provocation. This was more like break-ing in a bronco than riding an MTB!

Turning top-cogs now, Luke in hot pursuit, we zipped through a chicane, cleared a ford, then the trail smoothed so we put the hammer down, honking those high gears for extra power. I glanced

Nature, not the hand of man, carved this masterpiece known as Bowerman's Nose

DIRECTIONS

Start outside High Moor Centre, Princetown (GR590735). Head SO (SE) B3212 and up track alongside pub over South Hessary Tor for 2m to bridleway X-roads. Turn R (SW) on track for 2m to take R (W) fork into forest, swing L 0.4m down to Leather Tor Bridge.

SO (WSW then SW) bridge, cross leat to lane 0.5m away. L (SE) down to T-junction then turn R (W) for 2.5m past dam to T-junction. L (SSE) for 1.2m, SO T-junction, down to River Meavy and up to staggered X-roads. L (E), 0.5m to pass Ringmoor Cottage, then immediately R (E) 0.12m up to bridle-gates.

SO (ESE) (worn trail and new guide posts don't coincide) for 1m to waymarked bridle-gate. Fork R (SE) for 0.5m down through stream and swing L (ENE) to Ditsworthy House. L (W) then almost immediately R (NW) onto Edward's Path single track that contours (N) for 0.7m to corner of Scout Hut copse. Pass below 'hut' to T-junction.

R (ENE) 1.25m up track to Eylesbarrow buildings. Fork L (ENE) for 0.12m then fork L (NE) onto single track then track (NNE) for 1.25m to Nuns Cross. Swing L (NNW) past South Hessary Tor and back to Princetown 2.75m away.

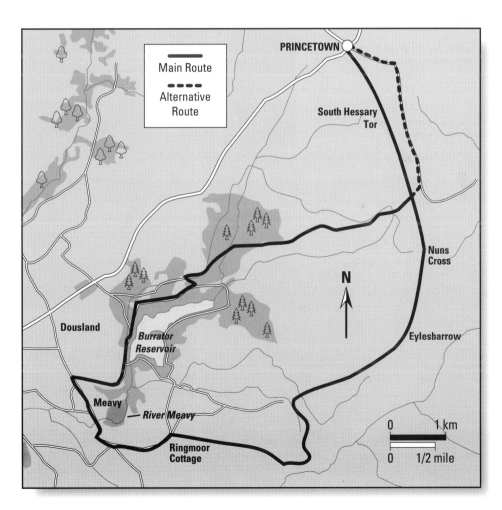

Burrator Reservoir glimmers behind the tiny hamlet of Sheepstor (above)

The Brendons are blessed with miles of all-weather bridleways (top right)

High above the vales of Exmoor you can experience some of England's best off-roading (right)

Idyllic woodland single-track in the Barle valley (below)

back and saw we'd left the others way up the valley. Reluctantly we pulled up and, with hands and hearts tingling, waited for the other two.

Waiting up turned out to be a wise move. A second, jagged, rubble-ridden stretch would have sorely tested our trail skills, had we hit it at speed. Beware when you're there and remember 'What you don't know, take slow!' We were lucky. 'Judder-Two' didn't last long and, with a turbo-boost from that wind, we sped on down to Burrator Forest where we took a track off right, deep into the heart of the plantation. Luke snatched the lead, I hung on his back wheel and we played 'close pursuit' through the trees to Leather Tor Bridge. A truly rustic river crossing if ever there was one.

We took ten, listened to the tempest roar through the pine-tops before pressing on towards Cross Gate. Luke, keen to demonstrate his youthful climbing prowess, sprinted ahead. An older trio, Pete, Dave and I, took the short climbs at a more measured pace and enjoyed the brief respite from that howling gale. And all too brief it was! At the forest edge we swung sharp left onto tarmac and into the teeth of that icy blast. Despite the steep descent we still had to pedal!

Burrator Reservoir, sporting a forest fringe and backed by Sheep Tor's craggy mount, could have been plucked straight out of the Highlands, yet here we were in the heart of Devon! The road cruise alongside the restless lake, past the dam and on down to Higher Meavy Bridge was much to Dave's taste; skinny tyres are his thing.

We were going to honk it up round Lynch Common by road but an off-road alternative, covered in fat-tyre treads and hoof prints, looked less daunting. The map showed a white track – ambiguous to say the least – but, as later enquiries revealed, there is no right of way. So don't do as we did; take on the tarmac! We took on the wind. It blasted down off the moor, numbing in intensity, forcing us into a heads-down, granny-cog slog up to Ringmoor Cottage. A spaniel, perched on the garden wall, watched our painful progress without interest. What a way to highlight our futility!

On past the cottage we fought the howling gale, on grass, up hill and I was reduced to wrestling with the wind for control of my front wheel. Determined not to submit to Nature's domination, I traversed a tortuous path up to a pair of bridle-gates. Gasping for breath, I turned to see the following trio trudging up the slope! They must have thought I was nuts to persevere with pedalling.

The gates were tossed to and fro in the tempestuous wind and we had to fight to keep them open. Catching it broadside for a time, we all leaned into the gale at a crazy angle. It looked bizarre! By the time we reached Ditsworthy Cottage we'd had it up to the ears with the wind. The furore had completely drained us and drowned out a flurry of rich, Anglo-Saxon expletives that were hurled into it! With relief we put our backs to it, missed Edward's Path in our hurry, and hammered down the track below Gutter Tor. Three bikers toiling in the opposite direction barely saw our fleeting form as, wind-assisted, we zoomed by.

I knew the climb up the broken cart track to Eylesbarrow tin mines. I'd careered down it in the summer but didn't relish the prospect of tackling it in the teeth of this storm. Needs must, and once up there at least we'd turn before the wind for the homeward run. It was that thought that kept the cranks turning until the mines were reached. A bit of R&R in the lee of a wall then we hooked up on some sinuous single track and forgave the wind. Propelled before it, we hammered down the gritty trail, hopping boulders, ditches and ploughing through pools of peat.

Once again Luke and I forged ahead until my wheel slammed into a granite slab, cunningly submerged in a peat bog. I executed an earth-sky-earth manoeuvre sans bike, kneed a rock, stopped and heard the bike slam down onto the slab next door. Ouch! Big, big chip on my pristine chainstay, warped bar-end and a dented knee. By the time Pete arrived we'd straightened the bar-end, winced at

Eyes down and let gravity do the rest. Brendon trail-blazing

the chipped paintwork and were ready to go. Happily we were just 150yds from Whiteworks Lane and a tiring Dave was directed onto it for his return to Princetown. It's also a wise move for you to use this road if the moor's wet.

Reduced to three and free to really motor before the wind, we made the most of the last couple of miles. With the final run-down to town empty – on gritty track bisected by three water runnels – Luke and I took our chance to top-cog it, clearing the ditches with a hop, skip and jump. Literally!

DOONE COUNTRY TRACKS

Distance: 28 miles. Time: 4.5 hours (dry), 6 hours (wet).

White-water fords shredded in arcs of spray. Sinuous single track – eyes down, bike skipping. Plus some high-speed tarmac chicanery by way of a contrast. Royal forest riding at its best.

Malmsmead (0.6m south of county gate on the A39) is a picture-book hamlet – a big gift shop really, hard by Badgworthy Water's renowned ford and packhorse bridge. Tourists abound but we could leave most of them behind to paddle in the river. (Mind you, the ice-cream's worth lingering for!) For bikers, Malmsmead offers the twin delights of car park and toilets plus a ford to play about in while your mates faff about. But Malmsmead has negative points too. In season it's seething with a mass of Doone-crazed loonies walking backwards, eyes closed and struck almost dumb by glutinous lumps of Devon cream toffee. With God-given trials skills you might survive in the throng but on high days and holidays it's best to choose a more remote parking spot such as Dry Bridge.

The first leg, Malmsmead to Brendon Common, coincides with a popular hack so I warned the other two – John and Luke – to look out for ponies as we swung left out of the car park, straight up a narrow road away from the river. It's a steep honk up to the summit of Postman's Lane to pick up the waymarked track where it heads south onto open moor. At last – off road again! The day is bright, the sea breeze cool and gritty track gives a heart-warming crunch as the knobblies leave tarmac behind.

In a burst of youthful exuberance, Luke raced ahead to take a long brown puddle at speed. Mud-laden spray dowsed the heather as he hit, bum aloft and honking hard. Spectacular it looked but with hindsight, tracksuit bottoms aren't ideal swimwear and a sodden Luke realised the wisdom in riding down a track's central ridge. Wrung out and rolled up on my rack (racks do have their uses), the tracksters were swapped for shorts and we were soon on our way.

**Cruising across Cornham Bridge
– the descent to it is eye-watering**

Just as well because with a lunchtime start and 25 miles to go we had to get cruising. A dip down through a stream brought us up sharp with a short, gritty climb out of its gully onto a flat-topped moor. Our cleft through the heather was one of many so we headed for a waymarker standing sentinel on the horizon.

It showed us to be on course for Brendon Common and, with no pony trekkers in sight, we sped on – Luke taking a more circumspect line when more water-filled ruts appeared. Our horizons closed in as the track dropped into a gully and all too soon we're on the tarmac of the B3223 and spinning for Simonsbath.

Several miles across bleak moor – here the wind gives us a welcome shove – where panoramic vistas open up. A dip into the weird wilderness of the Exe Valley at Blackpits and suddenly the knobbly hum is hushed. Super-smooth tarmac sets us all up with 'slicks' just as we hit the downhill into Simonsbath. A chicane has my rear rubber stuttering when a final bend reveals Birchcleeve Woods and our gateway to the Barle Valley bridleway. John overshoots – he must be a roady at heart – and is 100 yards up the road before he realises it was us back there.

The shade-dappled single track, weaving its way through the beeches, is in stark contrast to the roaring slipstream and blurred hedges that had just ended so abruptly. Still, slippery roots, followed by a short drop down to a track soon dispelled notions of an idyllic saunter, Pooh Bear style. Then we hit mud! Deep mud. Keeping hard by the hedge, we managed to power through and make firmer ground.

But the respite was brief. Twenty more yards of wall-to-wall glutinous sludge lay in wait. The epitome of politeness, I waved

Dunster Castle was built on this commanding site in the 11th century. The architect obviously had an eye for a picturesque setting

John ahead with a helpful 'Give it some stick!'. In true kamikaze spirit he crouched low and hammered down to the mire. His hubs sunk out of sight, the mud stuck, he stopped – a brief hover, legs akimbo, then... he just stayed there! Luke and I carried our precious metal across.

The ground was generally dry after recent droughts so I guess we'd not seen this bit of trail in its true colours! We picked up speed as the trail narrowed to contour the steep-sided Barle Valley and I thanked someone sensible for Crud Catchers.

A dramatic knoll – Flexbarrow, that's hard to credit to Nature alone – blocks the way. Here the trail cuts left above a deep cleft to swing round behind it and on past the remnants of the unsuccessful Wheal Eliza mine. On a dark night, more than a century past, a pale blue light hovering above its shaft led searchers to the wretched body of a murdered girl. Her father, driven by his lover's hate for his daughter, had flung her into the pit then fled to Wales. Caught, he was hanged in Taunton. Anyone for a night-time ride?

With a couple of ramps, bumps and bends to spice it up along the way we soon reached the foot of Cow Castle and peered into the dark pool at its base. Salmon, thick as a biker's calf, rippled the surface watched by small fry shoaling below the grassy bank; we all reckoned that a chance to slip into the cool waters would be great on a hot sweaty summer's ride. Idyllic. Who wants to honk on up the trail anyway? Well, we do.

Watched by a trio of walkers (of course we remembered to give way to them on the trail) we honked up steep grassy steps by the Cow impressing them – and ourselves – by making it to the top without so much as a tyre spin. There's nothing like a good tyre in the country! Down a grassy slope the path hugs the eastern ramparts of the fort, before dropping down across White Water Marsh to climb the Barle side of a lesser knoll. No prizes for guessing its name – the Calf. Negotiating the little beast proved tricky and just as I thought I had it licked, I careered off the side. Incredibly, I kept it together (or was it just that it didn't fall apart?) and made it back on course at the bottom.

I wasn't so lucky at Pickedstones (pronounced 'pickst'n') ford. I'm a sucker for water splashes and watching John cruise across had me itching for a run at it. So, with a 20 yards' start I dropped a cog and aimed for the distant shore. Great! Sun glistened off the spray arcing either side, I'm anticipating the achievement of a dry landing, then nothing. Stopped dead in the water by what foul trick? A rock had flicked up, knocked out my front quick-release, the wheel dropped out and bang! End of cruise. Luke, watching from the bridge, just laughed. OK, so next time I'll use the bridge.

Pickedstones is where we take up with the Two Moors Way –

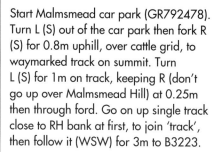

DIRECTIONS → → →

Start Malmsmead car park (GR792478). Turn L (S) out of the car park then fork R (S) for 0.8m uphill, over cattle grid, to waymarked track on summit. Turn L (S) for 1m on track, keeping R (don't go up over Malmsmead Hill) at 0.25m then through ford. Go on up single track close to RH bank at first, to join 'track', then follow it (WSW) for 3m to B3223.

Turn L (S) for 4.2m to Simonsbath. At bottom of hill, on LH bend, turn R (ESE) through bridle-gate into Birchcleeve Woods and fork R (SE) for 2.25m on bridleway, as it contours (mostly) down the Barle Valley going behind Flexbarrow Hill, past Wheal Eliza mine, then swinging L (ESE then S) behind Cow Castle and on to White Water and Pickedstones fords. There are footbridges here.

Turn R (SW) over River Barle on Two Moors Way track for 0.6m to Horsen Farm then SO (SW) for 2.9m to Blue Gate on county classified road. Turn L (WSW) for 140yds to turn R (NW) through waymarked gate (NW). Follow track for 1.5m, down over footbridge (the ford's a bit deep here) then bearing R up through gate and past Cornham Farm to B3358.

Turn L (NW) on road for 0.3m to gated sheep pen on right. Turn R (N) through both gates and follow trail for 1m as it zigzags first, then tracks NNW through gate, then NNE to another gate at field corner. Continue (NW) for 0.5m on vague single track to meet boundary fence, then swing R (E) for 0.6m, meeting track and passing through three gates, to Exe Head. Go SO (S) through last gate for 1.2m, presently alongside drainage ditch then the RUPP joins a footpath before dropping down over two fords onto the L bank of Hoaroak Water and contouring on to Hoar Oak Tree where the Two Moors Way goes its own way. Two gates.

Go through RH one for 0.75m, keeping alongside wall on your L then down through ford and swing R (NNW) up past building then on to gate. Continue (NNW) for 0.15m over next field on faint trail to gate in corner.

Now the mapped bridleway has no bridle-gate in the next fence so, ignoring obvious track, swing R (NNW) to gate 0.3m away. Continue (NW) for 0.5m over low hill to waymarked gate in far corner. Continue (NNW) on obvious bridleway for 1.6m across three fields to meet short bit of track to T-junction by Roborough Castle.

Turn R (ESE) for 0.7m, down over Hoaroak Water, up steep valley side then swing R (ENE) to sprung gate. Follow track (NNE) for 0.25m over brow and rejoining Two Moors Way on its track into Cheriton.

Turn R (NW) on lane for 0.7m, downhill then right at next junction following lane round LH bend over Farley Water and up steep hill to T-junction with B3223. Turn R (SSE)

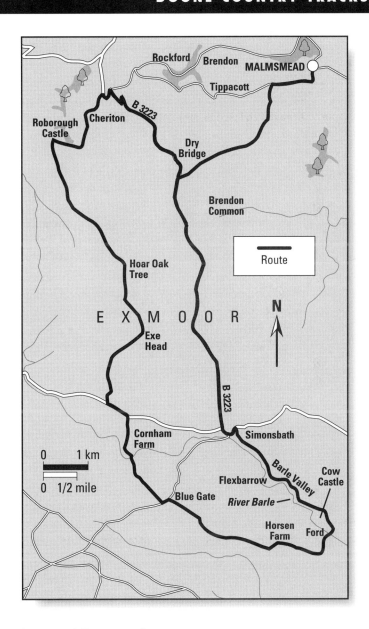

for 2m, uphill, to rejoin the Malmsmead bridleway on Brendon Common. Follow outbound route 3m back to start.

a footpath linking Exmoor and Dartmoor – as it heads north for Lynton. The map shows the track up to Blue Gate in white, but our hopes of it being all off-road were dashed at Horsen Farm. It marked the beginning of tarmac unclassified – nasty stuff! Never mind, the best was yet to come, only we didn't know it.

The brunt of that keen northerly began to tell as we neared the summit at Blue Gate and boy, were we glad to take a left into the shelter of a beech-hedged lane. But all too soon a waymarker by a gate signing 'Cornham Ford' marked a return to butting a head wind. The day was wearing on with the wind strengthening all the while so we donned fleeces – John had the wit to bring his wind-shirt – and put our heads down.

A decent descent was needed to buoy the spirits and Cornham delivered it right on cue. The gradient steepened, the track deterio-rated, crumbling into rock-filled gullies, and I blessed the staff at Ralph Coleman Cycles for conning me into a pair of Rock Shocks. The promised 'extra 5mph' came and went, the jolting faded, blurred trails and freewheeling were things of the past and I was really humming! A sharp right-hander bade caution so, against cruel temptation, I cut the speed and freewheeled to a stop by the river. Silence. The wait for the others was long enough to make me wonder whether they'd had a mishap. Happily they appeared soon enough and Luke was hungry to try the shocks. Guess that sounds a familiar scenario? Of course I said OK – later.

The ford looked much too deep – lucky I stopped then – and we pedalled across the bridge. The track wound its way through a cleft in the hillside, up to Cornham Farm and onto the B3358. Once again that cutting wind made itself felt as we followed the road then rutted track that zigzagged towards The Chains.

A gate delivered us onto Titchcombe Common – a pastureland which bore no trace of the bridleway's passing. In the far corner of the field, a gate beckoned. It proved to be the way to go but the bold trail that struck out beyond it split into a series of feeble foot-paths. Compass out and it's a long, north-easterly slog over grass to the boundary fence, with granny rings and a wandering mind the order of the day. Next to a strong head wind, grass is my least favourite energy sapper and today we had both!

Tired legs were glad to rest up on the short bit of track that drops down to Exe Head. Considering it's *the* river hereabouts, its source is a let-down. The imagined sparkling spring turns out to be a boggy patch of peat. Leaving the ignominious birthplace of the Exe behind, we continue alongside a meandering drainage ditch. Luke, tired of being thumped in the rump by lumpy bridleway, drops into the ditch. Naturally, we on the trail above threw down the mitt and it was race time. How he did it I don't know but, with

Exmoor's deep, oak-clad combes hide some sizzling descents

something akin to skilful bike handling, he beat us and was on the path ahead at the top of Chains Valley.

More gorge than valley, The Chains hide a trail that's cut out of the precipitous, turf-covered sides. Random rubble haphazardly strewn adds a touch of skip and it's bottomed off by two fords separated by a section of tricky bare rock. A feeling of Cumbria came all over me. Once again the shocks proved their worth, as I caught Luke on an open bend and the gap widened as the rough stuff got tougher. That tricky bare rock proved too much. The back wheel skidded away and I lost it. Too narrow to pass, the others landed in the stream behind!

Luke felt that such a brilliant descent deserved a second serving – with shocks of course. John and I sat by Hoaroak Water and tucked into cereal bars while he played Tomac. After I'd prized the bike from his grasp we took off down Hoaroak Valley – it still had a Cumbrianesque feel to it, like the 'back o' Skiddaw' – to Hoar Oak Tree, an ancient forest boundary marker. Here the Two Moors Way meanders off while we went on through a gate to cross some rough – literally – pasture to yet another ford. A building on the hillside ahead – Hoaroak on the map – sits right by the bridleway and acts as a convenient waymarker. Behind it a rubbly ramp puts traction skills to the test and then it's through a gate and back to grass.

With heads bowed to a wind that's gusting powerfully now, we struggle on to a gate in the corner and follow the track onto Furzehill's open moor. After a few hundred yards the track peters out. Then we meet an unbroken fence-line where a welcome bridle-gate should be! When I described the moor as being 'grassed almost entirely with hill-sized tussocks of Flying Bent' this is where I, at least we, found that out. By the time we'd eventually found a gate, our trusty Treks were so festooned with grass they looked more like Afghan hounds than MTBs.

Way off the route as marked on the map we went into orienteering mode, followed a compass bearing until an Exmoor National Park waymarker showed that our sense of direction was dead on. An obvious bridleway beyond confirmed that once again map and ground were in coincidence.

Three fields later we joined a behedged, muddy lane. Following John's advice on handling hoof-holed mud of the firm(ish) variety, I hovered my tail over the saddle and put on some speed. Bang! A log flicked up, locked up the front wheel and I grabbed air sans bike and bit mud! John had got his own back!

Turning right on a track T-junction brought us a glimpse of Roborough Castle. Not really a fort, the prominent, circular embankment probably sheltered an Iron Age homestead. More

INFO: EXMOOR

ACCESS

The venues for our routes are Malmsmead and Dunster. From the M5 Exmoor is clearly signed – from the north take the A39 at J23 and from the south take the A373/A396 at J27.

The nearest BR station is Taunton (Tel: 01272 294255) but, by cycling the 5m to Bishops Lydeard station at the terminus of the West Somerset Railway (Tel: 01643 704996), you can enjoy the 12m scenic rail ride to Dunster (or on to Minehead). It runs a regular service from March to October and bikes are free.

MAPS

OS 1:25 000 Outdoor Leisure 9 Exmoor; OS 1:50000 Landrangers 180 and 181.

mud, but thankfully dry enough to plug on through, finally turned to shale (loose, slaty rock). At a gate it dropped away, steep and narrow. Great! The occasional step gave a good excuse to loft the front wheel and, all in all, it was a short 'n' sweet fun run, round a nicely cambered left-hander and into the river. I nearly made it across but, as Luke pointed out from the stepping stones, fast and first isn't necessarily best!

The valley side looked near vertical from my vantage point in the river, but granny rings rule OK and we made it up onto Cheriton Ridge to rejoin the Two Moors Way into Cheriton. This is also a good alternative spot to park in the high season. Back to tarmac for a swift swoop down into the Farley Valley where we flashed by its little row of white cottages, only to be brought up short by a hairpin bend and a seriously steep climb to the B3223. Sometimes granny-cogging is excusable on the road!

The B3223 snakes up onto Brendon Common and hardly soon enough the familiar gritty track to Malmsmead hove into view. Cresting the short climb up Tippacott Ridge, the coast comes into sight and the scent of hot coffee and cookies is on the wind. The stone-ridden drop back into that first ford gives an upbeat end to our off-roading for the day. Then the tyres hit the hard stuff on Postman's Lane and start humming a 'Down the Hill Home' ditty.

BRENDON BASH

Distance: 10 miles. Time: 2 hours (dry), 2.5 hours (wet).

Knee-jerk downhills where tyres spit grit and hot blocks cream rims grey. These are the Brendon Hills. A quiet corner of Exmoor that escapes notice when your average, out-and-out, in-the-wilds type MTBer is perusing the Pathfinders. And because it's tucked away in the lumpy pastoral hinterland of Minehead, most tourists skip past it too.

INFO: EXMOOR

ACCOMMODATION

Not surprisingly this area is awash with hotels, B&Bs, campsites etc. There are several YHAs: Exford (Tel: 01643 83388) on central Exmoor, Minehead (Tel: 01643 702595) for the Brendons, and Lynton (Tel: 01598 53237) in the west. The Exmoor National Park (Tel: 01398 23665) provides an accommodation list or you can contact Minehead TIO (Tel: 01643 702634).

BIKE SHOPS

Ralph Coleman Cycles (Tel: 01823 275822) in Station Road, Taunton is staffed by a bunch of mad-keen bikers and will even rent you a steed.

NOTES

Exmoor is a very horsy area so be prepared to meet and give way to hackers. Remember that some riders are not so competent in the saddle and bikes will spook a frisky steed every time.

Start Dunster, Gallox Bridge (GR989432). From the Gallox Bridge return to the A396, turn L (WSW) for 0.2m to fork R and immediately take hairpin turn R (NE then NNW) for 0.5m up bridleway. At bridleway T-junction swing L (WSW) for 0.25m, still climbing. (Just as the trail levels there's a bridleway X-roads – by a little-used metal gate into a field – where you can take a left onto the open top of Grabbist Hill for a vista stop. Retrace your tyre tracks to the X-roads.) Then take a waymarked turn R (N).

Follow the track then single track for 0.75m, by field boundary for first 110yds then swinging L (NW) and L (WNW) again when the bridleway splits about 50yds further on. Pick up contouring single track into woods, through a final chicane to a broad track.

Turn R (N) then immediately take a hairpin turn L (W) – just about opposite the YHA's drive – over then alongside stream for 0.1m. Fork L (SW) back across stream for 0.12m along the edge of Staunton Plantation. Then turn R (W) for 0.5m up steep, technical climb to turn L (S) to a triangle of grass.

Keep SO (S then SW) for 0.75m, through S-bend and over track X-roads, to county classified lane. At the lane turn R (SW) then turn L (S) following the signs into Timberscombe village 0.5m away.

Take first L off the A396 into the village for 0.12m keeping L at

junctions to minor X-roads. Turn L (W) 50yds up to swing R (S) for 0.75m along tarmac drive to fork L (SSE) for 100yds up choked bridleway to bridleway track. (Do not be tempted to continue on drive then pick up the bridleway on next L turn.) Turn L (N) for 0.4m, through gate and up across field, to gate into forest plantation.

Go through and turn R (S) for 140yds then turn L (E) for 0.25m up to the county classified road. Cross onto deluxe forestry track for 1.75m, cresting the hill and over obvious track X-roads to a multi-track junction on Withycombe Common Hill.

Turn L (NW) then immediately L (N) again (ENP's blue daubs

used to mark the Luxborough–Dunster Way let you concentrate on the delights of downhilling) for 1.1m, crossing a forest road and onto twisty single track, to join Gupworthy Farm track.

Almost immediately fork L (NW) for 0.25m on single track (presently undefined but soon to be cleared by ENP) to rejoin Gupworthy Farm track – now a RUPP – on a hairpin bend. Then go SO (NNW) down RUPP 1.25m to Bonniton Lane. Turn R (N) for 110yds then fork R (NNE then E) for 1m up bridleway over Black Ball, down the side of Gallox Hill, past a row of picturesque cottages and on to the Gallox Bridge.

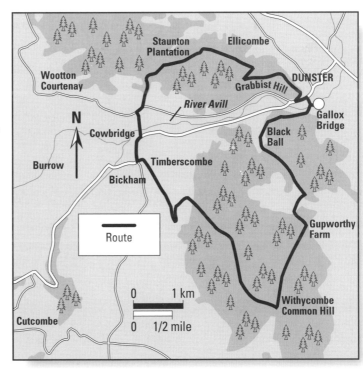

CHAPTER THREE

Downs of the South

THE SOUTH

South of the Thames estuary the landscape is particularly English. Rolling chalk hills, intimate valleys and acres of dun-coloured agricultural land that returns a golden heat shimmer in the height of summer. Such a lack of the obviously spectacular, often craggy heights that beset the western reaches of our island doesn't stop the south from furnishing us with some superlative off-roading.

Chiltern clay can get gloopy. This wallow's called Lily Bottom Lane

In fact the area is quite diverse, can definitely get radical yet provide some of the most picturesque venues and stunning views to be had from a bike anywhere. That's because the most MTB-friendly feature on the face of this fair farmscape are the great chalk ridges that finger their way westwards from the weald. Running roughly at 700ft downhills there are a few and the scenics are splendid.

Most famous of these 'fingers' are the South Downs that parallel our impressive Channel coast. A long, long time ago a warm sea here – much like the Caribbean today – was busily creating chalk from dead marine micro-organisms that fell like snow. Slow snow that is – 1in every 2500 years! At first pancake-flat, the South Downs are a geological ripple sent out from the ructions of mountain building beyond the Med. Steep on the north – 1:4 short 'n' hairy descents; gentle down to the coast – wind it up to 45mph in time. All are covered in miles of well-signed tracks and bridle-ways so you can spend weeks here and never repeat your route.

Just west of London the chalk and flint Chilterns – renowned for their majestic beech woods – rise 600ft or so above the Thames Valley. In their heart nestles Princes Risborough on the ancient Ridgeway, that's one of the oldest off-road roads in Europe. Brick built with a scattering of thatched ye olde dwellings, Princes Risborough is a Chiltern village providentially placed. Fortune has blessed it with all that an avid MTB trail-blazer requires: a BR station, good road access, local YHA, B&Bs aplenty and a pucker bike shop.

Unbroken, the Chiltern Ridge undulates south and west until the Vale of Pewsey thrusts a green and verdant finger between the ancient chalk uplands of Salisbury Plain and the Marlborough Downs. Either side of the Vale the mapped landscape is awash with Gothic script, mysterious mounds and enigmatic 'earth-works', all tastefully entangled in a network of ancient tracks and byways that are a joy to ride. Collingbourne Kingston, south of the Vale and up on the Plain, even has a forest full of single track by way of a refreshing change. Not surprisingly that's where we went to explore a couple of plain and vale excursions.

COLLINGBOURNE CIRCUIT

Distance: 19.5 miles. Climb total: 1800ft. Time: 2.5 hours (dry), 3.25 hours (wet).

A pot-pourri of high plains and deep, dark woods, Salisbury Plain is not all tank tracks and roller-coasting as two local lads, Steve and Barrie Planck, set out to show me on a double-loop of byway, trail and single track. It proved to be an ideal intro for what's on offer if you know where to look.

Start at Cleaver Inn – OK to park if it's a small party – (GR239559). L (N) 100yds then R (NE) for 1m through Brunton then R (ESE) at Spicey Buildings barn. 1m, keeping SO (ESE) at T-junction, to road then R (S) 200yds, L (E) on track 80yds to T-junction. R (SE) 1.3m, across valley and through woods, to track T-junction beyond field. L (NE) 1.1m to Scot's Poor then L (N) on road 1.1m over hill.

R (S, SE then E) 1.25m to X-roads above The Slay valley, R (SE) 0.5m to Hippenscombe Farm. L (S) 100yds through farm then quick L (E)/R (S) 1.25m over Little Down, SO (S) road, to RUPP T-junction. R (W) 0.9m, SO (W) road (watch out for wire across track down in dip!), to next road at Upper Chute. L (S) 80yds to T-junction, R (W then S) 0.25m to X-roads, R (WSW) 200yds, alongside green, to T-junction opposite pub. L (SSW) 0.6m, through R/L dog-leg, to T-junction by house at Coldridge Wood. R (SW) through barrier 0.5m to track X-roads. Bridleway ahead blocked so R (NW) 150yds to X-roads, L (SW) 0.25m to T-junction (easy to shoot through!) then L (S) 50yds to main track. R (W) 2m (there are single track detours round barriers), joining tarmac at 1.7m, to The Sheers X-roads. SO (WNW) 0.75m to A338 X-roads, then R (N) 1m to T-junction (easy to miss!), L (WSW) 2m on tarmac/track/tarmac to X-roads then R (N) on road 175yds to T-junction.

SO (N) 0.75m on RUPP track to Aughton Down T-junction, fork R (N) 0.5m to 'Black Barn' T-junction. Then R (E) 1.5m. Keep R (ESE) at T-junction at 1m, to A338. R (SSE) 0.6m to start.

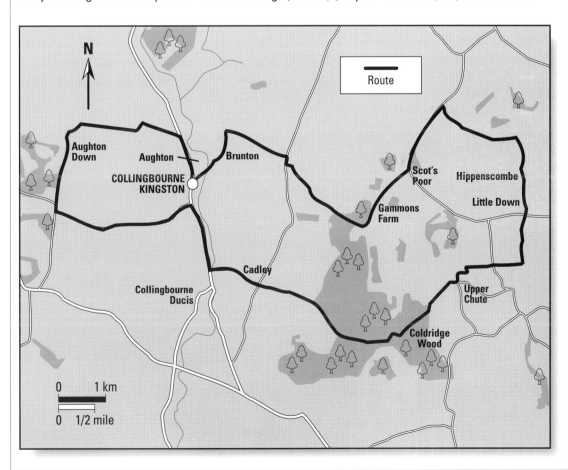

INFO: COLLINGBOURNE KINGSTON

ACCESS
Just 7 miles north of Collingbourne both Pewsey and Great Bedwyn have BR stations (Tel: 01734 595911 or 01672 62209) on the Reading–Westbury Inter-City route. Road access is on the A338 Hungerford/ Salisbury road running north/south between the A4/M4 and the A303.

MAPS
OS 1:50 000 Landrangers 173, 174, 184 and 185; OS 1:25 000 Pathfinders 1202 Ludgershall Hurstbourne Tarrant, 1201 West Lavington Upavon and 1185 Devizes Marlborough.

It was Saturday afternoon; hot sun, singlet, sun-block and sweat weather. Brilliant! A stiff climb up from Spicey Buildings gave us sweat-glistened brows and already the heat had got to Barrie; he took overlong to decide which way to turn and rode right into the ditch. But before long a bit of speed 'n' breeze had dispelled the heat-induced lethargy and we swept down through a dry valley – typical of chalk downland, so if you're a ford fanatic, and I'm a Ferrari man myself, forget it – and up into the cool embrace of Collingbourne beech woods. This is the local lads' playground but for now we were passing through to pick up a track that sweeps down alongside The Slay valley. The views were superb but as soon as the gravel track dipped, the gradient steepened, we took on speed and it was eyes down, pick a rut and race. We almost hurtled past the overgrown opening onto the sweet 'n' steep single track – single rut more like – off Haydown. Briars and bare arms made some painful encounters and the baked earth dealt out some bounce-back, but all in all we rated it an excellent exit off the ridge.

Zigzag through the farm – where we exchanged looks of mutual amazement with a trio of llamas – and it was into a calf-crunching, chalky-white climb up Little Down. Not so little! Today it was dust-dry but in the wet this is a real traction-teaser. Taken in downhill mode it has a reputation for doling out a murderous slip 'n' slide routine! What better reason for a return run this winter!

Back to flinty fast-track and a top-cog descent that dealt out a death blow to Steve's back tyre. My trusty Michelin Transalp/High-Country combo ain't exactly light but punctures are not a problem!

Puncture repaired and we swung west along a RUPP with low-slung wire waiting to whip those front wheels away. Happily a courting couple caused us to cut our speed and we spied the trap before it spiked us. Not nasty but nearly so! Into Upper Chute – where the Cross Keys is ideally situated to slake a summer's thirst – and beyond where we slipped into 46-12, spun cranks and sped down into the dark depths of Coldridge Woods. There awaited one of the highlights of the loop. Not on the planned route but ceded to us courtesy of a choked bridleway, where we detoured and dropped onto a sinuous section of single track in a sunken ditch. Steve and Barrie blasted off, dust clouds billowed off the berms as they disappeared into a haze of flickering shadows and sun shafts. Caught napping I kicked cranks hard, carved into the corners, careened off the berms and breezed through a bevy of chicanes for a brilliant run. Too short! Too sweet! I was sorely tempted for a rerun and, in retrospect, regret our pressing on.

A fallen tree in Collingbourne's Cowcommon Bottom treated us to a second detour onto more single track in between the trees. Essence of MTBing! It was a shame to quit the forest, but Steve had a last blast downhill lined up before a pub stop at the bottom.

INFO: COLLINGBOURNE KINGSTON

ACCOMMODATION
Manor Farm (Tel: 01264 850251), The Cleaver Inn (Tel: 01264 850368) and The Blue Lion Inn (Tel: 01264 850358) are local B&Bs. More info available from Marlborough TIO (Tel: 01672 513989).

BIKE SHOPS
Elite Cycles (Tel: 01264 850869) at Unit 1, Bourne Works, Collingbourne Ducis.

Golden Ball Hill high above Pewsey Vale is one helluva climb but the views are verdant (left)

An enigmatic sign on one of Europe's oldest roads – The Ridgeway (below)

DIRECTIONS → → → → → PLAIN AND VALE LOOP

Start at Cleaver Inn – OK to park if it's a small party (GR239559). R (S) on A338 0.3m to T-junction (easy to miss!), R (WSW) 2m on tarmac/track/tarmac to X-roads then R (N) on road 2m to Down Farm. L (SW) 0.2m up track to X-roads, L (S) 0.3m to X-roads, swing R (WSW then SW) 0.8m. Keep L (S) 0.25m to A342 tank crossing.

SO (S) and immediately fork L (S) onto bridleway track 1m to T-junction in valley bottom, R (SW) 1m to Baden Down Farm T-junction then L (ESE) 0.25m, past barn, to X-roads. R (WSW then S) 0.5m to T-junction, swing R (W) 1.6m to road at Longstreet (last 150yds can be skid-row!). R (N) 0.3m to Enford T-junction, L (WNW) 0.2m over river to A345.

R (N) 1.3m to West Chisenbury Farm then L (WSW, S then W) on Ridgeway track 1.4m to T-junction with unmetalled road. R (NNW, NW then W) 3.8m to Chirton Maggot bridleway T-junction.

R (NNE) 1m to T-junction then keep L (NW) 0.25m to A342 X-roads. SO (N) 4.5m (take L into All Cannings for pub 'n' shop) to road/gated RUPP X-roads. SO (NE) 0.8m to T-junction, L (N) on RUPP track 1.25m, swinging R (E) and keeping S of Wansdyke earthwork, to field. L (E) 275yds then L (N) through bridleway gate, immediately R (SE) 200yds on RUPP grass track to gate. SO (ESE then SSE) following fence line 0.7m to road.

SO (SSE) 170yds to gated T-junction with bridleway. L (E) 0.4m, by Knap Hill, to gate then SO (E) over fields along Golden Ball escarpment edge for 1m to signpost. Swing L (NE) 0.2m to gate, SO (ENE) 0.3m on track to X-roads, SO (E) 0.25m up to T-junction then R (S then ESE) 0.75m to house on Huish Hill.

L (N then ENE after dog-leg) 0.6m on RUPP to A345 X-roads. SO (S then E) 0.4m into field then L (NE) 0.3m to T-junction. L then R (N then E), on Martinsell Hillfort embankment 0.25m, through gate, to copse edge. (Embankment was choked so we back-tracked alongside the embankment where it turned south, then L through a cutting, L alongside field for 150yds then the path dropped L back onto embankment and original route.) Swing L (NE then ENE) 0.5m, round copse then

alongside adjacent wood, to road.

R (ESE then S) 2m, keeping R(S) at 1st and 2nd T-junctions, to New Mill T-junction. (Keep SO to follow wet weather route.) R (W) 0.75m to B3087 staggered X-roads. R/L (SSW) 0.75 to stream then SO (SSE), with hedge on your R, 0.25m to bridleway gate beneath pylons.

SO (SSE) 0.5m, passing through barn/windpump enclosure, then L (ENE then SSE) 0.6m up track to field corner. R (SW) 0.2m to bridleway gate, hairpin L (NE then SSE) 0.5m, back along fence then down to track junction. L (NNE) 1m to T-junction, R (SE then SSE) 1.75m, past barn, up to Aughton Down T-junction. L (N) 0.5m to 'Black Barn' T-junction R (E) 1.5m, keeping R (ESE) at T-junction at 1m, to A338. R (SSE) 0.6m to start.

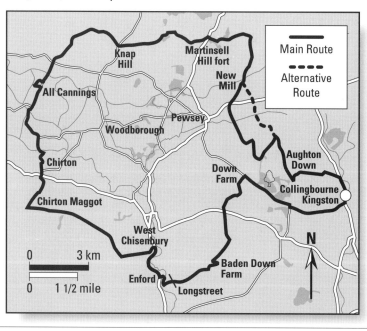

0   3 km

0   1 1/2 mile

N

Start from Mountain High Cycles, Princes Risborough (GR 809034) and take Loosley Row/Speen road (SE) off roundabout for 0.4m to Kop Hill T-junction. Then L (ENE) for 0.75m climb to T-junction. R (SE) 0.6m to take meandering bridleway R (SW) for 0.7m through Hillock Wood to T-junction, then L (SE) 20yds on drive to go SO (SE) on road for 0.4m to bridleway/lane X-roads.

R (SSW) on bridleway 0.3m to Lily Farm T-junction then L (SE) 0.6m to pick up narrow bridleway off L (ENE) for 0.6m into woods and SO (ENE) to X-roads. SO (N) on lane 1m through Gt Hampden then L (WNW) onto Hampden House drive then track for 1m to cross Grim's Ditch earthwork.

Swing L (W) then R (NW) for 0.25m descent to track. R (NE) 10yds through gate then L (NW) off track for 0.75m past Green Hailey farm to road. R (NW) 0.2m to go R (N) through Whiteleaf Hill picnic site and past viewpoint for 0.5m to T-junction. Then hairpin R (ESE) behind club house for 0.4m to road at Lower Cadsden (pub stop).

R (E) 0.5m over hill, just beyond gate, to pick up narrow bridleway off L (NW) for 160yds then R (ENE) on bridleway path for 0.5m to road. L (N), past Buckmoorend, for 1.9m to go R (NE) at T-junction 0.6m to car park on RH bend at Low Scrubs.

SO (NNE) on bridleway track 0.4m to T-junction, fork R (ENE) 1m to road then SO (NE) 0.3m to X-roads in Wendover. R (SSE) on A413 1m to T-junction, R (W) for 0.4m to T-junction by farm then SO (W) on bridleway track for 0.75m to bridleway T-junction. L (S), past pub, 0.25m to bridleway/road X-roads in Dunsmore then SO (S) for 1.2m to Cobblershill road.

R (S) then immediately R (W) again onto bridleway 0.6m across valley to road to go R (NNW) 0.8m, past pub, to road

end/bridleway X-roads. SO (NNW) on path to R of road (there may be felling operations here), 0.5m down to T-junction then L (W) 0.2m to road at Buckmoorend. SO (W) on road then bridleway to retrace outbound route for 1m to road. R (NW) towards Lower Cadsden for 0.3m then fork R (NW) on bridleway for 1m, to A4010. L (S) on RUPP track, road and bridleway track SO (SSW) at X-roads, T-junction and X-roads for 1.7m to bridleway/road X-roads. R (NW) to return 0.25m to start.

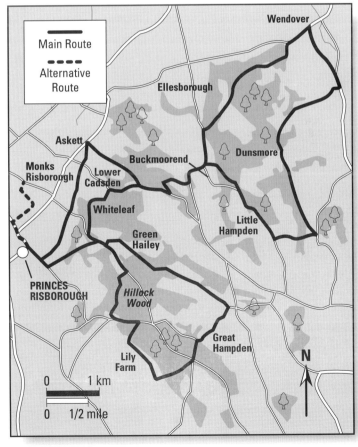

Main Route
Alternative Route

Wendover
Ellesborough
Askett
Monks Risborough
Lower Cadsden
Buckmoorend
Dunsmore
Whiteleaf
Green Hailey
Little Hampden
PRINCES RISBOROUGH
Hillock Wood
Great Hampden
Lily Farm

0   1 km
0   1/2 mile

N

Why wait? Barrie slipped in ahead, creamed through the chicanes so fast that only some desperate hedge flaying kept me on his tail. And those hedges hurt! The Sheers pub is the best place for some R&R before taking on the second leg of the loop up on Salisbury Plain proper.

High plains drifting with a dash of roller-coasting took us over Aughton Down for the high-speed dash through 'Black Barn Bend' and to the top of the final run home. In familiar race-for-the-finish mode Barrie and Steve picked a rut apiece and sped away with me, trying hard to stay in touch. A radical left-hander nearly caught me rut-hopping but the rubber hooked up, saved the day and I careered through, spitting grit and spinning out on the straight run home. Wide-eyed and breathless we cruised into Collingbourne in pasta-killing mood!

PLAIN AND VALE LOOP

Distance: 42 miles. Climb total: 2750ft. Time: 5.5 hours (dry), 7.5 hours (wet).

A heady mix of fast-track trails – the epitome of Salisbury Plain spinning – with a dip across the Vale of Pewsey for a scenic repast and radical riding that'll give you an entirely different perspective. And a challenge. This ride would have anyone's calves begging for a break!

TRIPLE TRACKER

Distance: 21 miles. Climb total: 1950ft. Time: 3.5 hours (dry), 5 hours (wet).

A trio of tree-covered circuits over the convoluted contours of the Chilterns.

INFO: CHILTERNS

ACCESS

From the M40 exit at J4, (High Wycombe) and follow the A4010 Aylesbury road, or exit at J6 and take the B4009 north via Chinnor. From further south take the A404 from Maidenhead to High Wycombe; from the north either go via Aylesbury or use the M1/M25 anti-clockwise to gain access to the M40, J4.

Princes Risborough is on the BR Marylebone line (Tel: 0171 222 1234); bikes are OK except at 'peak times'. For Inter-City info try BR Reading (Tel: 01734 595911).

A Chiltern cart track cuts through England's green and pleasant land (above)

Golden Ball Hill's bridleway is part of the 250 mile Wessex Way off-road cycle route (right)

Shafts of sun filtered down through the high beechwood canopy, painting a play of light and shadow dance over the forest floor. Late bluebells spread a cool haze through open glades, gentle zephyrs rustled leaves and carried the song of a thrush between the trees... A group of clay-clad cyclists dropped over the edge of a slick, cream-coloured slope masquerading as firm forest single track. Tyres bloated, tread blocked, grip gone and the crocodile file of bikers disintegrated into a free-for-all slalom slide. A slide that pitched them all, pell-mell, into a tree! Bar one rider. First over the top, he slid serenely on. Oblivious to the chaos and mayhem behind!

And that about sums up the Chilterns. The wonderful serenity of cycling through sun-dappled woodland, interspersed with short 'n' slick, slippery drops over greasy gloop and roots. Mud-pluggers' paradise! All born of a week of dark clouds and deluge that dissipated into a day of sunshine when we got dialled into the first big climb of the day – the Kop Hill calf-stretcher. Idyllic summertime weather but the ground beneath was slurping about in the depths of winter. Clean machines got an instant mud-caking down Lily Bottom Lane and to the tune of scuff 'n' scuff of brake blocks on rims, we dived into the undergrowth of an overgrown path, all but disappeared, then emerged into open-gladed beech wood.

A multi-directional arrow painted on a tree pointed every which way but ours – straight on. Straight on to some twisty single track between pine trees, all rooted, wet and wonderful. A brief sojourn on tarmac took us past the stately facade of Hampden House – home of Hammer horrors – and onto cart track across the fields. Occasionally they get ploughed up, but the path alongside Grim's Ditch is both a haven and a heaven-sent alternative. Back into

INFO: CHILTERNS

MAPS
OS 1:25 000 Explorers 2 Chiltern Hills North and 3 Chiltern Hills South; OS 1:50 000 Landrangers 165 and 175.

ACCOMMODATION
The local YHA is at Bradenham (Tel: 01494 562929 or 01895 673188). For B&Bs, hotels etc. contact the High Wycombe TIO (Tel: 01494 461000).

BIKE SHOPS
Mountain High Cycles, Princes Risborough (Tel: 01844 274260). The staff are all keen cyclists and organise regular guided rides.

Salisbury Plain in summertime. Hot enough to seek out some cooling slip-stream (above)

ACCESS

Regular trains run from London Victoria
(Tel: 01273 206755 or 01705 825771) to
Arundel. Road-wise the A27 coastal route
gives east/west access and the M23/A23,
the A29 or A24 puts London just 50-odd
miles due north.

MAPS

OS 1:25 000 Pathfinders 1286 Cocking
Sutton and 1287 Pulborough and Steyning.

ACCOMMODATION

Everything from a National Trust bothy
(GR962119) at Gumber Farm Barn
(Tel: 01243 65313) to high-class hotels.
There are plenty of YHAs but Warningcamp
(Tel: 01903 882204) is the nearest. Arundel
TIO (Tel: 01903 882268/882419) has details
of alternatives.

BIKE SHOPS

Arun Bicycles (Tel: 01243 537337) at
30b Southgate in Chichester. For hire bikes
Arundel Cycle Hire (Tel: 01903 88371).

woods Sean, our local guide from Mountain High Cycles, took the
lead, shouted something about getting into granny-cog mode when
you hit the pit and shot off. I tail-ended the group down a tasty dip,
clicked into 12-26 and hit a horrible little climb-out, saturated and
riddled with roots. But the gods smiled down on me that day and
I made the top without a dab. Feeling dead chuffed, with ego
inflated, I cruised on, straight onto a narrow path of pot-holed
clay that turned the bike into a bucking bronco with skates on! I
fought hard but the bike won; I dabbed and my challenged ego
deflated faster than a burst balloon.

Whiteleaf Hill – site of a famous chalk cross with mysterious
origins and of unknown age – was where that pell-mell wipe-out
occurred. But we hadn't learned our lesson and tried a re-run further down. This time only the lead man did a mudslide then he was
ploughed into the dirt by the others hot on his heels. They'd been
unable to brake! He and his bike were fast becoming a homoge-
neous 'grey with a hint of clay' colour.

Sean had cunningly kept the climbing to roads with sections of
single track and track slipped in between. In the dry there's plenty
of opportunity to take it fast and furious, finessing in and out of the
trees, hopping roots and playing the fun element for all it's worth.
Today the saturated soil slurped incessantly, tyres slipped and the
constant battle for traction added a technical edge that, in polite
company, I wouldn't dare admit to enjoying.

Downhill dashes were few and far between. The gradient was
there but then so was the gloop. Even the final run-down to the
Aylesbury Road, described by locals as a demonic descent, was
reduced to a mud-caked, granny-cog slog through a glutinous bog.
Mind you, that was exceptionally dire as well as disappointing.
The rest I actually enj...!

CHILTERN CRACKER

Distance: 40 miles. Climb total: 3000ft. Time: 5 hours (dry),
7 hours (wet).

Hit the dirt on some sweeping classic, dry valley descents and
enjoy a saunter along England's oldest coast-to-coast off-road –
the Ridgeway – before upping the adrenalin factor on single track
that dips and dives between the boughs of majestic beech trees.

WING OUT OF WHITEWAYS

Distance: 28 miles. Climb total: 2800ft. Time: 4 hours (dry),
5 hours (wet).

A roller-coaster ride of clay hardpack or saddle-bound
mud-plugging depending on the season. It's fast and furious for
the fittest only.

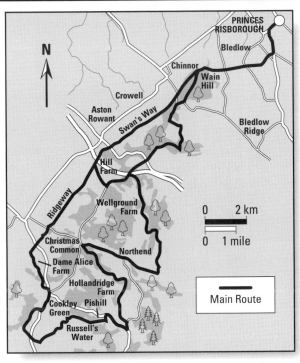

L (S) 130yds then R (W) on bridleway 0.25m down to T-junction. L (S) 0.2m to go R (WSW) at T-junction for 1m, SO (SW) following signs at Redpits Manor then keeping L (SW) at exit to Priors Wood, to road. SO (WNW) 0.2m to X-roads, SO (NW) 0.4m to fork R (NNE) at bridleway sign for 0.7m.

R (E) 0.25m to Cookley Green T-junction then L (ENE) on B481 0.6m to X-roads, L (NNW) on B480 200yds then L (W) at T-junction for 0.2m. Fork R (N) on bridleway track for 0.9m then split R (N) at Dame Alice Farm on track 0.25m to X-roads.

R (NW) on RUPP (road then track) Ridgeway/Swans Way for 3.3m SO (NE) at all junctions to familiar Hill Farm X-roads. R (SE) 0.8m up to go L (NE) on road for 1.75m. Over A40 X-roads, to go SO (NE) onto bridleway drive on LH bend.

After 25yds fork L (NE) on bridleway track for 0.9m down to T-junction then fork L (E) for 200yds to bridleway/track X-roads. L (NNE) up steep bridleway, ignoring L fork at 0.5m, for 0.7m to Crowellhill Farm drive then R (N) 20yds to lane. L (WNW then NNE) 0.9m to fork R (ENE) for 0.4m to T-junction.

Take bridleway drive L (N) 0.4m to Chinnor Hill turning bay. L (NW) 10yds then R (NNE) 0.75m to Wain Hill X-roads. R (E then SE) on Ridgeway to return to start on outbound route.

Start from Mountain High Cycles, Princes Risborough (GR 809034) and take A4010 (SW) High Wycombe road 1.1m to X-roads with Upper Icknield Way. R (WSW then W) for 1.6m towards Bledlow, SO two X-roads to 3rd X-roads with bridleway track. SO (W) 1m to Wain Hill X-roads with Swans Way track.

Now swing round L (SW), contouring at first, for 4.2m, under M40, to Hill Farm X-roads (tea garden stop). L (SE) 0.8m up to go L (NE) on road for 0.75m to start of metal crash barrier. R (NE) on bridleway alongside RH barrier 200yds to bridleway gate. SO (SE) for 0.8m descent to bridleway gate. SO (SSE) and dismount for 0.2m walk to Wellground Farm X-roads. Take 2nd R turn SO (SSW) on bridleway drive then track at T-junction 0.6m to track T-junction.

Keep L (S) 0.6m up bridleway to turn R (S) at X-roads on hill top for 0.25m, SO (SSE) track 0.2m to lane. R (S) 1m, on lane then signed bridleway keeping L (SE) at 0.5m and R (SW) at 0.9m, to road. (If you end up on neat tarmac drive turn back S to road.)

R (WNW) 2.5m to T-junction with drive at Christmas Common. L (SSE) 0.3m then L (E) 0.2m to swing R (SSE) for 2.8m gentle descent, through Hollandridge Farm, to road. R (S) 0.25m to B480 T-junction then R (NW) for 0.8m to turn L (S) onto drive in Pishill for 0.2m. Fork L (SSE) on bridleway 50yds then R (W) 1.25m, keeping to edge of wood, through farm to pond at Russells Water.

Woodland scenes don't come much more majestic than those created by the Chiltern beeches (above)

A delightful carpet of fallen leaves but on South Downs single-track they can be wickedly slick (top)

Wending a way through green fields of corn in the Chilterns

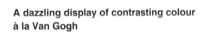

Flying along the South Downs Way in winter (above)

A dazzling display of contrasting colour à la Van Gogh

DIRECTIONS → → → → →

Start Whiteways Lodge car park (GR002108). NNW on bridleway track to R of kiosk, keeping L at next two junctions as bridleway swings to W, for 1m. R (NNW) on The Denture 1.4m to bridleway X-roads, R (N) for 200yds to Stane Street sign post.

L (W) for 150yds to X-roads. SO and (WNW) for 1m, passing masts, down rutted track to bridleway path off R. Keep NNE (not ENE) then N across valley, over Farm Hill to X-roads 0.9m away. SO, keep N alongside wood, over Barlavington Down as track swings NW then NE down into woods and X-roads 0.7m away. L (WNW) for 200yds, hairpin R and follow zigzag track down to A285 400yds away.

R (N). Road sweeps L. Go SO onto Beechwood Lane (dead end). After 0.9m bridleway track starts gentle roller-coaster W for 1m (ignore L forks uphill), to multiple X-roads. L then keep R (SW) and climb 0.5m up Graffham Down to South Downs Way (SDW).

R (W) for 2.1m, passing tower hide in field on R, to bridleway X-roads. R (NNE) across field, into wood on tricky single track then track down Heyshott Down to T-junction 0.75m from top. R, 75yds, R again for steep, rutted climb SE up to bridleway X-roads on SDW above Charlton Forest. (For shorter, wet-weather route L here and follow SDW for 4.75m to Burton Down bridleway X-roads.)

SO (S) for 1m through forest. Track swings R (SW), past fork on L and building on R, to Charlton 1.6m away. L on road for 150yds then R for 100yds to take bridleway on L.

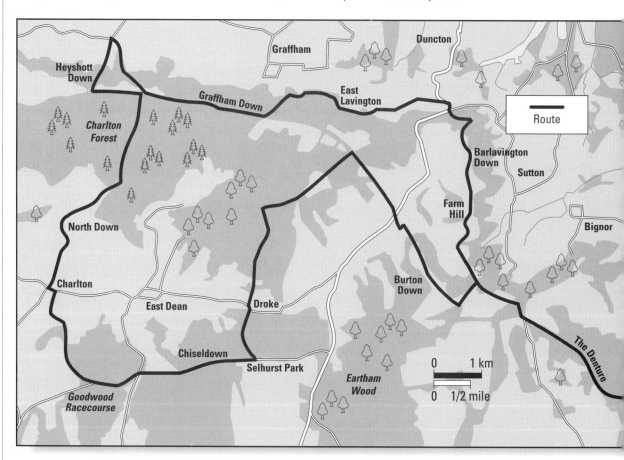

S for 1.3m, up by Goodwood racecourse, to lane. L (E) and shadow lane on single track for 0.5m. Rejoin lane at X-roads. Continue E on tarmac for 0.5m to woods, pick up parallel track on L for 1m then L (N) on bridleway track down to Droke.

L on road, 75yds, R through gate and up track, single track and track heading N/NNE for 1m climb to T-junctiion. L (N) on main track, 500yds to X-roads. 1st R on grassy track E, out of forest, along its edge then cross field to SDW 1.5m away. R (SE) on signed SDW for 2.5m, past Littleton Farm on A285, to bridleway X-roads at Burton Down. L (NE) towards masts. 0.4m R at T-junction (now back on outbound trail) for 0.6m then swing R (S) for 220yds to bridleway X-roads. L (ESE) then SE, on The Denture again for return to Whiteways 2.2m away.

The South Downs were formed from ruffled sea-bed to create some superlative mountain bike terrain

**The graphic contrast of back-light enlivens a
Chiltern woodland in winter**

The wind roared through the treetops. Above, rain clouds
scudded across a darkening sky, on the leaf-covered track below
two mud-caked bikers, locked in wheel-to-wheel combat, raced
through the empty forest of Duncton Hanger. Flints, icy wet,
glistened in the slick clay on a narrow bend. The two hit it at warp
speed, legs trailing speedway style. Both bikes slewed through the
apex, hit roots on the outside, fought for traction then crash! The
trailing rider wiped out, ploughed a furrow through the leaf litter
and fetched up in a bramble patch. Still astride his steed.

Seconds later we arrived. Our South Downs guide Jake, still
down and desperately trying to extricate himself from the tangle;
Alistair, his brother, in vertical velocity, honking back up the trail
to see where he'd lost his friend. And this was typical. For these
two guys there seemed to be no such thing as taking it easy.
Always on the edge, mostly at warp speed, they were supposed to
be guiding us over their favourite trails. We hardly saw them!
Luckily we touched base enough times to be sure we were doing
the same rides. I should have guessed it would be like this when
we met up at Whiteways Lodge car park.

Overnight Nature threw a reeling corkscrew of bad weather at
the south coast. So with a wet nor'-westerly in our faces we set off
for the radio masts by Bignor Hill. Boy that wind was cold! First

A Wessex Way trekker pedals into the sunset on Fyfield Down near Pewsey

fun of the day – a bit of decent gravity pull in other words – had Alistair and Jake vying for lines down a well-rutted chalk track. Then it was onto clay single track. A skid-pan alley with long-armed brambles grabbing sleeves and slewing bike and rider round with exasperating regularity. Happily this was short-lived and we emerged onto open field – appropriately named Farm Hill. Four in line and all leaning at a crazy angle into a fierce side wind, we still had to crank it hard downhill. Alistair had warned us that our calves would be begging for a break before the end. Mine were already!

Duncton Hanger's crooked descent – one of Alistair's choice bits of single track – plunged down through the forest to the A285. Determined to grab the lead he motored off, Jake in hot pursuit. And that's where we first came in – on that bend. A quick dust-down – scrape-off more like – and it was off again, skipping and skidding on a deadly mix of leaf litter and clay. It wasn't a case of picking lines so much as slurrs!

A brief tarmac sojourn on Beechwood Lane below the northern face of Downs' chalk ridge provided a mud-discard opportunity, then it was back to track. We roller-coastered westwards. Jake tried to limbo below a branch, fell and nearly got flattened by Alistair hot on his heels. At Graffham Down we knuckled down to some hard graft – a 375-foot climb-out. Slick flints and clay made traction tricky, but the radical rubber wrapped round my rear wheel dug right in and I drove on up in fine style. As ever Jake and Alistair led us up and then had enough verve left to take air on every little bump the South Downs Way offered.

A brief ridge ride gave us a welcome respite from the eternal fight for traction, so it was almost with regret we dipped north off the Way at Heyshott Down. Another of Alistair's fave descents, this one kicks off off-camber, followed by a dip under a low-slung yew tree. He warned us not to hit it at speed. Then he blasted away at warp-factor 9, Jake right on his tail! He was right though. A case of 'don't do as I do but do as I say'. Heyshott's a delight and, despite the gruelling climb back up to the Way, I'd have been happy to go at it again. Not today though!

We spun cranks eastwards along one of England's oldest by-ways, blasted down the open expanse of Littleton Down and into Upwaltham Valley. In error we missed the Way, motored down Littleton Farm's track where I was nearly decapitated by a lethal strand of barbed wire. Lying in the dirt, a split second having saved me from disaster, I couldn't help but laugh. Nor could the others. No sense of responsibility these bikers!

With one more long climb to conquer – and at last Jake had the decency to show signs of fatigue – up and over Sutton Down we crossed the A285 again and put our heads down. Then the familiar radio masts hove into view and signalled the long downhill home. I allowed myself an inward smile. A bit of gritty chicane, just past the masts, furnished a brief taste of technicality before we zig-zagged back onto The Denture, where it was a case of winding up to a crank spin. This time I managed to keep those two speed merchants in sight. That is until we got to within a half mile of the café. They vanished! By the time we got there hot coffee and chocolate cake were already in hand.

RIDGE RIDE RETURN

Distance: 20 miles. Climb total: 2200ft. Time: 3hours

An all-seasons, all-weather blast along the South Downs ridge from the 20th-century ring of Whiteways roundabout to the 2,500-year-old ring of Chanctonbury Hill fort – and back. Cows, hikers and hackers permitting, it's a breeze with views on top and all the work's built into four climbs – the one out of the Arun Valley enjoying the status of being the most serious on the South Downs Way!

Humming down the highway – the Ridgeway where it hugs the Chiltern hills

DIRECTIONS → → → → →   RIDGE RIDE RETURN

Start Whiteways Lodge car park (GR002108). L onto A29, head N for 0.75m. R (E) on South Downs Way (SDW) bridleway by Combe Wood. 0.9m SO lane on new bridleway, over new Arun Bridge, 75yds then L away from river. Follow bridleway, over railway, up to B2139. R (S) for 220yds, first one side of B2139 then the other, then L (NNE) up SDW road. 0.5m on L up SDW bridleway.

Keep to ridge on obvious, signed SDW for 5.5m to A24. Cross with great care – 70mph motors blasting by here! Rejoin SDW bridleway track for 0.9m climb to T-junction. L (NE) for 0.5m to Chanctonbury Ring. Return to Whiteways on same route.

The Ridgeway River – a legacy of winter's wet

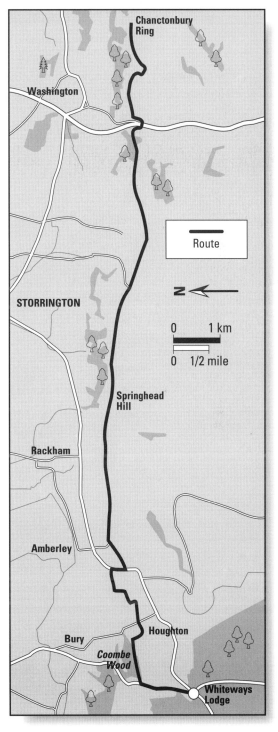

Midshires and Marcher Hills

THE MIDLANDS

The south and west Midlands contain a rich diversity of landscape that provides some of the country's finest off-road riding: the Welsh Marches with their remote, heath-covered hills, where gritty tracks fly off their flanks for some prime-time descending; the Cotswolds – an elevated limestone plateau criss-crossed by ancient tracks and cut by combes to form a roller-coaster landscape that's full of surprises, not least the abrupt bluffs that soar above the Severn valley. Then there's the Forest of Dean; epitome of the secret single-track setting, the Dean is a mountain bike Mecca for Midlanders, and justly so.

The Cotswolds

Archetypical England. A rolling countryside full of green byways, honey-coloured cottages and ever so nicely National Trustish. Heart of England weekend break country where a jolly 'Hello' and a hack over the hills with nothing but a hip flask for company is par for the course. There's plenty to entice and entertain the beginner, but if summertime pootling is an anathema to your off-road expertise, then try our route that trips along the famous Cotswold Edge – it's a bit on the wild side for the Wolds.

The Royal Forest of Dean

Hit the dirt in the Dean just once, taste its unique mix of fast fire-road and serpentine single track, and you'll be back. Again and again!

It's an intoxicating blend that'll whet the appetites of BMX bums, hard-core hard-packers and hazy-day leisure riders alike, as they explore the plethora of paths that wend their way between the boughs of one of Britain's largest broad-leaf forests. A forest that sits high on a remote plateau between the Severn and Wye rivers.

INFO: COTSWOLDS

ACCESS

The elegant town of Cheltenham boasts a mainline BR station, so you can actually get there with your mates and the bikes. It's a good idea to book about a week in advance through your local BR booking office. By road the north/south link is provided by the adjacent M5 and the east/west route is facilitated by the M40/A40 combo.

MAPS

OS 1:25 000 Pathfinders 1043, 1066, 1067 and 1090 or OS 1 inch:1 mile Touring Map 8 The Cotswolds.

ACCOMMODATION

Cotswold country is liberally peppered with places to put your head down, from camp-sites through to luxury health farms. Contact Cheltenham TIO (Tel: 01242 522878) for details.

Cleeve Common on the Cotswolds – a Mecca for local MTBers

The valleys are steep-sided and deep – eyeballs-out descents to titillate the nerve ends of the exhibitionist, the hill tops broad-shouldered and flat. Ideal for a fast cruise in the flickering light of a sun-dappled fire-road. The Royal Forest of Dean is every biker's ideal off-road venue.

Long Mynd

On Shropshire's western fringe, where it meets Wales, the gentle farmscape rucks up against the Cambrian Mountains. The ruffles create an Alpinesque landscape of intimate proportions – not too far up but plenty of hairy hammertime down. Known as the Long Mynd Hills and made of pre-Cambrian volcanics, they're the oldest bit of England. Like real mountains, these hills are incised by ravine-like valleys where sinuous single track waits to test trail skills and tempt providence. On top, acres of purple heather hide red grouse and, lying secluded in the bracken, numerous springs gush crystal-clear water. There's something for everyone: short, sharp, long, loose, easy, fast, slow, slick, trick. Together with their western brethren, the Stiperstones, these hills have got the lot.

HELL OF THE NORTH

Distance: 34 miles. Climb total: 4000ft. Time: 6 hours (dry), 8.5 hours (wet).

Grab your wheels, take a ride on the wild side and get your mind warped on a radical Cotswold caper.

As Chris, one of my guides for the ride, said: 'This descent's brilliant! A straight blast down through the forest.' Great! I slicked in 12-46, spun the SPUDs and sped off into timberland. Slip-stream roared like Landrover rubber, the bike went bronco on rut and rubble as gravity got a grip and I hurtled through Lidcombe Wood's dark embrace. This was ace! Just enough dip 'n' dive to shred the edge of the envelope and no surprises in store. Until I hit a track crossing.

The down-side had a hump, the back wheel flicked off the top, the bike kicked butt and I nose dived! I hung in there – just! No elegant manoeuvre à la Hans Rey, just a white knuckle grip and a fear of getting my teeth gritted! Suddenly it's another track, hump and a second heart-stopping skid, hook-up and adrenalin kick. Still the slipstream roared. A couple of dices with disaster and suddenly we're the untouchable trail-meister. Foolish when my fly-time finale's in a wipe-out with alarming regularity! Next time we meet a bump there's more finesse to the flight. Airtime's under control and we're really humming, picking lines and slipping from side to side on a divine track between the trees. Is this MTB heaven or

INFO: COTSWOLDS

BIKE SHOPS

Cheltenham's a bit of a two-wheel town so there are loads of bike shops. Two that come recommended are Cheltenham Cycles (Tel: 01242 255414) and Bike-Tech (Tel: 01242 251505). MTB hire (and accommodation) is available from the Cotswold Cycling Co (Tel: 01242 250642) at 48 Shurdington Road, Cheltenham.

One of the Cotswolds most famous landmarks Broadway Tower; this folly was occupied up until 1972

what? No! It's a demonic descent from the 'Hell of the North' and the penultimate plummet on our loop! 'Hell of the North'? Sounds like Cumbria or the Cairngorms? No – we're definitely in the Cotswolds and the 'Hell of the North' is a 62-mile sortie by well over 1,000 bikers bursting for a mud-bath and a beatific grin in the face of winter's adversity. It's a *randonnée* with a reputation – no race but an outright mud-plug with the occasional downhill flight to flick off the grime.

Also out for today's excursion were two lads, Steve and Tony, from the Cotswold Cycling Co, and Chris's partner on life's great

Stone clitter and cylindrical bales litter a bridleway near Salperton on the Cotswolds

DIRECTIONS → → → → →

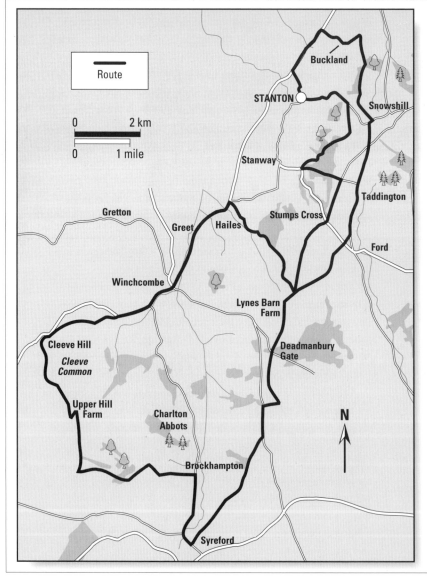

byway, Jacquie Stanton, all rustic and rural, saw us head out and up onto the Cotswold plateau via a trick piece of tarmac that climbed curvaceously contour by contour. A timely warm-up without the tease of traction-testing. Once aloft, we were in for a undulating spin with mud, track and tarmac interleaved in unequal proportions with a spot of 'Inter-City grass-whip' – straight, single track descent through deep grass – to spice up the 10-mile pootle to the top of Sevenhampton Down.

Time to break out of bumbleland with gravity-assisted, gate-free track to get the blood pumping through the veins! Chris kicked out in front, me close behind, we picked a rut apiece and spun cranks for over a mile of

HELL OF THE NORTH

Start Stanton car park (GR067344). L (NNW) 0.6m then R (NNE) 1m on B4632 to turn R (ESE) 0.75m, through Buckland, and fork L (NE) after S-bend. Climb 0.75m, on tarmac at first, to T-junction after gate. Keep L (S) and follow RUPP 1.5m to T-junction then turn R (WSW) 50yds and turn L (S) 300yds to barn. Zigzag L/R by barn to continue (S) by field boundary 0.25m to road X-roads.

SO (SSW) 2m to X-roads then R (SW) 2.1m, keeping SO (SW) at junctions, to Lynes Barn T-junction. Turn L (SE) 200yds to gate past last barn then R (SE then S) 0.25m, field boundary on your R, to gate past woods. SO (SSW) 0.75m to Deadmanbury Gate then L (SSE) 120yds and R (S) back on track 1.2m past Roel Mill farm to road.

Turn R (W) 0.25m then L (S) at X-roads 0.5m to keep R (SW) at fork 1.2m to road/gated RUPP X-roads. SO (SW) 1.6m to road/RUPP X-roads then R (NW) 0.25m and R (N) again 1.75m towards Brockhampton to X-roads.

L (W) 0.8m to T-junction, R (NW) 0.3m to T-junction with RUPP by diddy shed then turn L (SW) 0.4m to gate. Don't go through. Turn R (W) 1.2m, through another gate and watch out for bog in valley bottom, to join tarmac up to X-roads with green. R (N) 1.2m to bridleway gate, then L (W then N) 80yds to trees then track zigzags, R/L/R down hill to gate 0.25m away. SO (N then NW) 200yds, R (N) up onto roughly contouring single track 0.5m to gate on Cleeve Common. SO (N) 0.5m, dropping L (WNW) by post before Cleeve Hill fort then contouring R (N), to track at Nutterswood.

R (N) 0.6m (you can follow rough track loops off L) to track T-junction. SO (NE) 0.6m, passing close by road and WCs where you swing R (ENE), to clubhouse. Keep contouring R (ENE then E) on obvious track 0.6m to T-junction then L (ENE) 0.5m down to B4632. R (E) on main road 3.5m, through Winchcombe (café stops here) and under railway to T-junction.

R (SE) 0.75m, keeping L through Hailes (tea room here), to bridleway track off L (ESE). Climb 1.75m up track to join tarmac and onto road/bridleway X-roads. Hairpin L (NNE) on bridleway 1.75m to bridleway/road X-roads at Stumps Cross then keep SO (NNE) 1m to bridleway/road T-junction and L (WNW) 0.8m down to road.

Hairpin R (ENE) up bridleway track 0.4m to multi-track junction in valley bottom. Swing R (NE) 0.75m, up obvious track with stream over to your R, past Parks Farm to take bridleway off L (NE) 275yds across field to bridleway gate. L (N) 0.7m to gate onto junction with tarmac RUPP. Fork L (NW) 1m, SO staggered X-roads with Cotswolds Way, on gated track into Stanton. Keep L (W) 300yds down to T-junction then R (N) 100yds to start.

INFO: ROYAL FOREST OF DEAN

ACCESS

By road from the north the M5/M50 to Ross-on-Wye then take the B4234 straight to our kick-off point at Pedalaways in the Cannop Valley. The A40 from Gloucester is the main gateway from the south and east, then take the A48/A4151/B4226/B4234 to Pedalaways. From South Wales use the M4/A48 link to Lydney then the B4234.

Let the train give you a pain, try to book your bike(s) and let BR whisk you right to the Forest edge at Lydney. Ring BR Gloucester (Tel: 01452 529501) for details.

MAPS

OS 1:25 000 Outdoor Leisure 14 Wye Valley Forest of Dean.

ACCOMMODATION

Bespoke accommodation by the bedroomful abounds in the Forest itself. From camping – try the Forest Enterprise campsites (Tel: 01594 833376) – to multi-star hotels. The Coleford TIO (Tel: 01594 836307) has all the details. The Dean's YHAs are at St Briavels (Tel: 01594 530272) and at Welsh Bicknor (Tel: 01594 860300).

smile time that's tricked out with a sweet chicane at the bottom. Chris was in training mode, attacking every adverse gradient with a vigour that had my legs over-heating in an effort to keep abreast. Not sensible – we had a long way to go! Steve and Tony had promised some radical dip 'n' dive single track up on Cleeve Hill and with names like Nutterswood adorning the map, I couldn't wait.

Panoramas opened out west as we breasted the escarpment along Cleeve. A tableland that's the Severn Vale lay spread out a thousand feet below. Isn't it great to be way up high just knowing that there's a phenomenal plunge in store? This one's a real twister. It flip-flops off the top then hits a radical right with a deep berm, where the centrifugal force just sucks the tyres into Mother Earth with a slide-defying grip. But for the gate, we'd have shot through a deep ravine, full of free stone, far too fast to pick up the climb-out right and then taken a plummet into Presturby by mistake. Following the Cotswold Co. boys we contoured round Cleeve Hill, tipped off the edge on stepped single track that's a touch technical, but safer than Swissair if you accidentally take time out from gravity.

Down at the clubhouse we took ten by the tee for tea before our trusty Cotswold duo departed – duty called. Cleeve Hill had a final, riotous rut 'n' rubble run in treat before we departed for Winchcombe. No wonder it's where the locals go to loon about! With Winchcombe we were treated to a carbo load of the monoxide variety when we got sandwiched in a vehicle queue. Yuk! (Ignoring the traffic, Winchcombe's ideal for a final pit-stop before hitting the last few hills.) Up ahead was the hill out of Hailes, and with 25 miles already under the belt I looked up at the tree-clad climb with a certain unease. Chris struck out in the lead and disappeared from view. I was content to play tail-end Charlie until I realised we had just one more climb to go. I made an all-out effort to reel him in and failed by about 500 yards! Can't win them all.

All that height gain put us at the top of that demonic 'Hell of the North' descent – where we first came in – for an eyeballs-out ricochet off hard-pack humps that set the heart pounding and etched an ear-to-ear grin. But this wasn't the last drop off the escarpment edge. Another arduous climb was dialled straight in. The toughest test of traction and climbing tenacity of the trip – 500ft that kicked off with a mud incline that stressed tired muscles beyond imagining, quickly followed by a steady granny-cog slog up rutted forest fire-road. The legs slowly built up a head of steam. For a change I was lead man but I hate the pole position, especially with Chris hard on your heels, angling for a line past and pushing you to your limits. I focused on the rough track a few yards ahead, picking lines with care, not daring to glance back and cursing

Start Bourton-on-the-Water (GR160210) at T-junction with A429. Go SO (W) onto bridleway 0.75m over fields to T-junction beyond wood at Aston Farm then R (NNE) 0.6m to road. L (NNW) 0.2m then R (NE) at T-junction 0.4m, L (NNW) at T-junction for 175yds then R (ENE) 100yds into Upper Slaughter.

Fork L (N) – not to the church –

100yds. Before river, turn L (W then N) 0.8m to climb valley side up past cottage and down to track T-junction. Turn L (N) 100yds to road. L (WSW) 0.25m to turn R (NNW) up bridleway drive ('Private road. No vehicles') 1.6m, keeping L (NNW) at fork after 0.5m, to road at Chalk Hill.

Turn R (E) 1.6m to X-roads with Condicote Lane track then L

(NNW) 1.5m, SO all junctions, into Condicote. Keep L through village then fork R (N) just after Cedar Gables Farm for 1.2m to T-junction at Hinchwick Manor.

SO (N then NNE) on bridleway that goes R (E) of woodland 1.25m up dry valley. Then zigzag R/L, effectively SO (WNW), 0.6m on single track through copse, to road. L (WSW gradually to WNW) 3m, SO all junctions, to bridleway/road X-roads by Park Farm. R (NNE) 0.5m to take RUPP off L (N) for 1.25m to gate onto junction with tarmac RUPP. Fork L (NW) 0.9m, SO staggered X-roads with Cotswolds Way, on gated track into Stanton.

Keep L (W) 300yds down to T-junction then L (S) 3.2m. Fork L (S) at next T-junction beyond village then SO (S) B4077, to B4632. L (S) then immediately L (SE) again 0.75m, keeping L through Hailes (tea room here), to bridleway track off L (ESE). Climb 1.75m up track to join tarmac and onto road/bridleway X-roads. L (ENE) on road 0.75m to T-junction (easy to shoot by!) then R (S) 0.4m to fork L (E) for 200yds walk to swing R (SSW) and join bridleway 1m to road. R (SSW) 0.4m to X-roads, L (E) 0.75m to road then L (ENE) to Kineton (good pub) T-junction.

R (SSE) 1m to take bridleway track off L (ENE) on right bend. Follow bridleway 1.2m, it swings immediately. R (S) then L (ENE) at gate, to road. L (NE) 1m, SO junctions, to pick up outbound route at Chalk Hill.

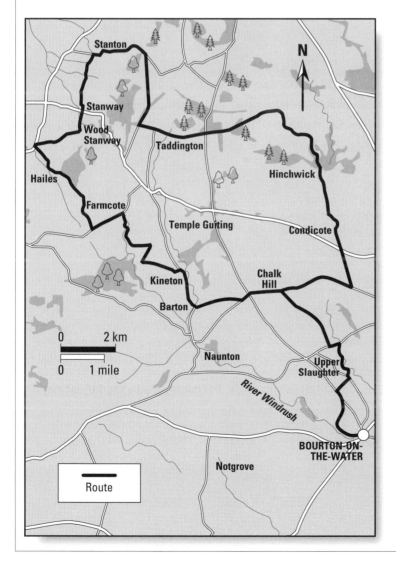

Clear views over the Forest of Dean are few and far between. Puttemage's vantage point offers fine vistas

DIRECTIONS → → → → →

Start at Pedalaways (GR607125). Exit car park at NW corner onto main track for 1m. Bear L (NNW) for 0.3m up through barrier then L (W) at T-junction beyond. Contour through Sallowvalets 1.2m to hairpin R (W then S) turn. Ignore paths off L; continue 0.6m to A4136 barrier at Edge End.

L (SSW) on path for 0.5m to X-roads at Worcester Walk. SO (SSW) 0.4m and SO (SE) at X-roads near Mile End for 0.25m then swing R (SW) 0.3m round N,W and S sides of camp-site perimeter. Turn R (WSW then S), almost back on yourself, 0.2m to B4226 near Broadwell.

SO (S) past the 'Dippies' 0.2m to pick up power lines by sub-station. Keep SO (S) for 1.25m on track, dropping down to C road N of Dark Hill on single track. L (S)

200yds to T-junction. R (W) 0.4m to X-roads then L (SE) 0.25m to fork. Take trail off L (NE) 250yds round boundary to track junction by fenced edge of old quarry. Ignore trails off L and R, go SO (E) down trail that curves R (SE then E) past the 'Doughies' to swing R (S) 1.1m to Parkend Walk junction. Quick L/R (S) onto footpath track 0.25m to X-roads. SO (SSW) to climb 0.3m then L (E) at junction 0.3m to C road. SO (E), keeping to L (N) side of buildings. Ignore L (NNE) fork, keep SO (E then S) for 0.3m to multi-X-roads in Parkhill enclosure. A quick L (E), R (S) and L (SSE) then follow track 0.5m to go SO (E) B4234 and railway (NE).

Climb 0.6m to forest edge. Swing R then turn L (NE) for 0.6m (ignore tracks off R) to C road barrier. SO (NE) into wood 0.5m joining C

road in front of Rising Sun pub. At track/road X-roads go R (SE) over dismantled railway, climbing 0.75m beneath power lines up to Cockshoot Wood. L (NE then ENE) for 1m first alongside boundary, then round Danby Lodge to drop straight (ignore L and R forks) down to C road T-junction at Blackpool Bridge.

SO (NE) 250yds to take track off L (NW). Keep climbing and keep R (NNE) 0.5m then turn L (SE) 0.4m round spur (views over Blakeney Walk). Go R (N) to climb 0.5m to gate and stile. Go over. SO (WNW) to multi-track junction. Take second L then swing R (WNW) on footpath track 0.2m up to Staple-edge bungalow. Go round to NW corner of boundary. Do not drop down R, keep SO (N) along summit then descend (N then NNW) down all the way to

cross dismantled railway) 1.1m to picket gate. SO (NNW) past Lightmoor workings to join dismantled railway and Family Cycle Route. We're following this in reverse so take care.

Keep SO (N) on railpath for 2m. Turn R (N), leaving railpath, to climb 0.3m to track. Turn L (WSW) 1m along ridge, past café, to barrier. Go R (W then NW) to drop 0.4m ignoring all trails off R. Then ignore L fork, keep SO (S) descending 0.25m to railpath. SO (S, E then NE) 0.4m round spur then take hairpin R (S) down to second railpath route. SO (S) 1m. Hairpin R (NNW) 0.2m back to B4234 opposite start.

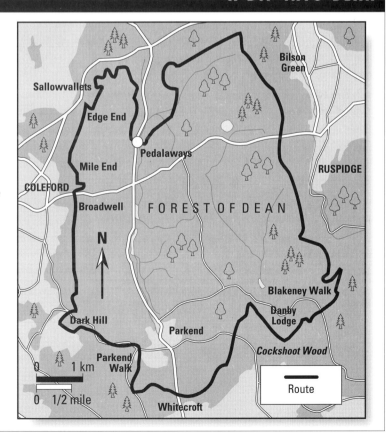

INFO: ROYAL FOREST OF DEAN

BIKE SHOPS

Revolution (Tel: 01594 833330) in Coleford carry out repairs, true wheels and carry a good stock of kit. They also hire MTBs as do Pedalaways (Tel: 01594 860065), who operate from the start of all our routes in the Cannop Valley. Their café is an MTBer's Mecca, so if you want to strut your stuff, get friendly with other lycra-clad loonies or simply enjoy the yummies, call in.

NOTES

The Forest Enterprise here (Tel: 01594 833057) understands how to integrate the fast-growing sport of MTBing into the grand scheme of things. To make its job easier, please follow the Off-Road Code, keep off single track when it's wet and respect the needs of other visitors. Access to many of the Forest of Dean routes are permissive only and may be revoked at any time. Telephone the Forest Enterprise for up-to-date information.

A word on your whereabouts. If your map-reading skills are rusty then my advice is to employ a local guide.

Chris's pursuit with every painful second. Up around a bend the track went exponential and I just about died on the spot! Still I could sense Chris right on my tail. I sat on the saddle nose, the treads tore at the track for grip, spitting grit in heart-stopping salvos that sent the legs into after-burn. If I'd been behind I'd have backed off by now. I glanced up ahead. Safe passage on my side came to an abrupt end. I dreaded scrabbling across the scree that lay scattered across the middle of the track. Defeat at the eleventh hour, the summit just 20 yards away! Summoning a last milli-watt of power, I accelerated for a do-or-die dash across the track. The back wheel slipped, pain seared up my legs as I tried desperately to control the spin, it stopped, the tyre gripped and I was home free! Dead. Blown out! But ecstatic to have conquered that climb! And Chris? He was nowhere to be seen!

A mechanical had put paid to his bid for pole position and it was nothing more than a furtive imagination and an ego to inflate that had me conquer that hill! With the last climb dispensed with we revelled in relax mode – warm-down is the technical word – before dialling into the last ditch descent of the day. Watch it when you go – there are two gates which'll put a glitch in your trip if you don't take care!

BOURTON BASH

Distance: 35 miles. Climb total: 3000ft. Time: 5 hours (dry), 6.5 hours (wet).

A pot-pourri of pootle, rad, track and road that should please most of the people most of the time.

A DIP INTO THE DEAN

Distance: 22 miles. Climb total: 1600ft. Time: 3 hours (dry), 4 hours (wet).

Ring around the Forest with detours to delight.

Not wishing to be the subject of a Forest Rescue Team call-out, I enlisted the help of local guide, artist, biker-extraordinaire, old man of the Forest and rescue crew member Jeff Phillips, together with tandemaniacs Chris and Jacquie Marley from the local MTB club. Jeff took one look at my OS Outdoor Leisure map and laughed. Apparently what's etched in ink ain't what appears between the trees, and everyone knows that forest is an orienteer's Armageddon. So we consigned the map to the bumbag, followed Jeff's tyre tracks and were rewarded by some of the finest forest riding in Wyevern.

To our delight, the sullen skies that darkened the Dean disintegrated under a determined springtime sortie from the sun. About time too! Still, unbelievers that we are, we were all steaming beneath winter kit by the time the barrier at Sallow Vallets was reached. Chris even had full gloves on! A quick stripdown and then we dipped off the track onto some genuine single track that twisted and turned between the trees. I hummed a discordant 'Robin Hood', listened to bird-song in harmony and drifted into a springtime muse – until a low branch clocked me one. Better watch the trees as well as the trail!

Back to track for a quick burst of speed – actually springtime reveries had us all in saunter mode – and then Jeff led us back into the trees over what appeared to be the spoil heaps of an old mine. Get some 15ft speed bumps, add a random selection of roots,

D I R E C T I O N S → → → → → WYE VALLEY WANDER

Start at Pedalaways (GR607125) and follow 'Dip into the Dean' to X-roads at Worcester Walk. Turn R (W) 250yds to cross B4028. 100yds into wood turn L (WSW) on path 0.2m to junction. R (N then W) 0.2m to A4136 at Ninewells.

L (SW) 100yds then R (NW) at track/road X-roads for 300yds to join lane. SO (NW) then swing L (SW) past school to T-junction 0.5m away. L (SW) 100yds to B4432 X-roads. R (NW) for 0.4m to Christchurch. Road swings R (N), go SO (W) 0.3m on C road to

edge of forest and Forest Trail. Turn R (N) into woods then almost immediately L (NW) down drop. Keep SO (NW) 0.7m descending rocky gully to track. R (ENE) up round L (W) hairpin for 2m roller-coaster run to T-junction. L (N) 200yds (watch out for cars!) into Symonds Yat car park.

L (N) onto C road for 150yds, under footbridge, then hairpin L (SSW) to descend 0.4m to Wye on bridleway. SO (SW) for 1m then L (S) for 2m climb up Coalpit Valley. Keep round L (NE) for final 0.5m up to C road at Berry Hill.

SO (E) for 0.5m keeping SO (ESE) until the A4136 at Five Acres. L (NE) 0.5m to familiar road/track X-roads. Care here! Go R (SE) 0.4m, SO (SE) B4028 then swing L (E/ENE) 0.25m. Turn R (SE) at X-roads near Mile End to follow the 'Dip into the Dean' route home.

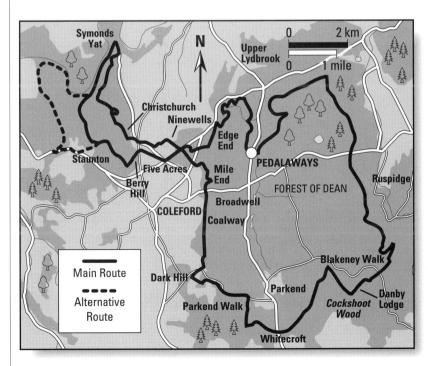

Main Route
Alternative Route

Clinging to the sliver of single-track,
that sweeps down Minton Batch on
the Mynd (above)

Take a BMX circuit, blow it up to MTB
proportions and that's Lightmoor deep
in the Dean (left)

Autumnal mists paint a sylvan scene
over the Wye valley

Down to Asterton. A Long Mynd descent
with a twist in its tail

branches and stumps and it's playtime. Great stuff but Chris reckoned the 'Dippies' – a medley of bomb-holes, ramps and ruts said to be the birthplace of off-roading in the Dean – has more to offer and we're no more than a mile away. Why wait? Chris and Jeff dropped off the spoil heap, Jacquie and I followed, slip-sliding on roots and leaves still wet from the recent rains. The Forest's not so tame as I'd imagined!

Down in the 'Dippies' – just off the B4226 at Broadwell – the local trio sped round, taking air, twisting and turning like a bevy of boys on BMXs until the inevitable wipe-out after taking it too fast, too close through an off-camber bomb-hole. Moral of the tale: don't tail-gate your mate through a big dip. We continued on through the forest.

Power lines were our guideline along the expansive summit of Purple Hill, then the track dropped away for some well-earned hammertime on a bit of rubble and hard rock. Superb but short-lived. A road to cross. A slick, black tarmac snake thrusting through these secretive glades, we darted over its pristine surface like a band of Cherokee across a railroad. The maze of pathways covering Dark Hill confused the eye, but Jeff – without hesitation, deviation or repetition – led us through and into the 'Doughies'.

Ideal tandem territory, the Dean has miles of forest road to explore...

The 'Doughies'? Quite simply the most sensuous bit of sinuous single track that's been designed by, ridden by and loved into the dirt by MTBers. Need I say more! Split into sections and slipped in between the trees, it's a tortuous trail that dips and dives, slots in the odd drop-off and bomb-hole to create a rhythmic ride, where it's 'don't think, just do' or you're destined for a session of diabolical dab, dab, dabbing!

The Doughies spewed us out into the dappled light of open forest road, adrenalin coursing through our veins and well into the elation of a fast-track descent through Parkend Walk. But down-hilling isn't where it's at for everyone – to conquer a tricky climb has its own just rewards – and the stepped shoulder of Oakenhill, still slick from early morning rains, tested power control and technique to the limit. The hill top is open – bleak in bad weather I guess – but the prize for cresting it is a compulsory pub call at the Rising Sun at Moseley Green. But the penalty for pub-time over-indulgence was indigestion beneath the power lines that climb up Cockshoot Wood. I actually got hot!

Past a stretch of exposed Roman road – they missed the bridge but we didn't – then a second steep climb up woodland pathway for a return to track. Late afternoon sun skipped the light fantastic across the expansive view over Blakeney Walk, so we took ten and admired Nature's (and man's) handiwork.

... or on the off-road trails, in a group

Loitering on a hilltop was not Chris and Jeff's idea of off-roading. The delights of the deserted Lightmoor workings were tugging at their tyres. Pick a BMX track, pump it up to MTB proportions and that's Lightmoor. It's a Mecca for locals and a mind-blast for MTBers with an edge to shred. Big drop-offs, chutes and jumps, you could play away the whole day there and depart shaky-legged and drunk on adrenalin. Me? A return trip is already booked!

To round the day off, we hooked up on Forest Enterprise's own Family Cycling Trail for an eventide saunter through a sun and shadow land, that's a forest in spring. Idyllic or what?

WYE VALLEY WANDER

Distance: 32 miles. Climb total: 2600ft. Time: 5 hours (dry), 7 hours (wet).

Wing it out to the Wye Valley to test your MTB mettle.

THE DEVIL'S DETOUR

Distance: 30 miles. Climb total: 2300ft. Time: 4.5 hours.

A real pot-pourri of lane, track and single track – not really technical but fast in the off-season – with two miles of down-hiller's delight as a just dessert.

INFO: LONG MYND

ACCESS

There are BR stations at both Shrewsbury (Tel: 01743 364041) and Church Stretton – book at least a week in advance for a hassle-free rail journey. Church Stretton is 14 miles south of Shrewsbury on the A49. Unless you're coming from way south or west then via Shrewsbury is the easiest route.

MAPS

OS 1:25 000 Pathfinders 910 Church Stretton, 909 Montgomery and 888 Welshpool or OS 1:50 000 Landrangers 126 Shrewsbury and 137 Ludlow Wenlock Edge.

ACCOMMODATION

On the west side of the Mynd there's a YHA at Bridges (Tel: 01694 771296). Campsites and B&Bs can be contacted via Church Stretton TIO (Tel: 01694 723133) or through the Ludlow TIO (Tel: 01584 875053).

We kicked off with a couple of miles of tarmac-cruising; flicking through autumn sunlight along shade-dappled country lanes. Then Brendon and Roger, two lads from the local MTB club acting as our guides, led us off the lane for our first taste of Shropshire dirt. A fine piece of forest road that delivered us onto the Mynd's long ridge. A panorama of the Welsh Marches lay spread out below and it was hard to imagine, with the scent of heather so heavy in the air, that in times past we would have been standing in a forest. Loitering in the middle of a main road! This was the ancient Port Way.

Today traffic up here would have terrified ancient travellers – it hurtles skyward with a banshee wail then... silence. Up above a glider climbs, quick as a swift. A few hundred yards to our right the Bronze Age track is not so much Port Way as Run Way.

We opted to miss out on playing chicken with planes and dropped off the western slope on a grassy, spur-hugging single track. Smooth, straight and fast, at first the tasty opener was deceptively simple – this bridleway had a sting in its tail. A tail it kept well hidden. Suddenly we crested a steep, water-scoured ramp bottomed off with a 90° left. In another time, another place, it could have added spice to a Grundig circuit!

There's nothing like some gravity to get the heart-strings singing and we set off for Medlicott in high spirits. Even a leaf was excuse enough for a hop! A bit of mud-plugging where the tarmac looked little used and on to some high-speed roller-coaster riding, that brought us to Bridges and from there we had a long haul up to Stiperstones car park.

Above us lay the jagged ridge of rocky outcrops known as the Stiperstones. Legend names the Devil as being the careless architect. Such a fascinating outline, steeped in myth and legend, just begged to be ridden, but the bridleway straight up from the car park was a dead-end and we wanted to loop. We chose to access the ridge from the Hollies up an entertaining bit of bridleway that had us ping-ponging off the path at regular intervals. But once we got up there the panoramas from the top were fantastic so we kept to the ridge, kept the views and put the hammer down (walkers permitting).

Down by Blakemoorgate we got lost in a fallow field – the local lads were none too familiar with trails this far from home. But your intrepid guide soon pinpointed the spot on the map (actually we stopped right next to a Nature Reserve info board with 'You are here' printed in the middle), and we pushed on. Firm track took us down to Brook Vessons Farm and out on to another lane for a brief encounter with tarmac before we took up with an old county unclassified that contours a valley head before

Take the B4370, SW from Church Stretton (GR453938), 1.5m to Little Stretton X-roads (a few yards on there's a little church worth a look). R, round LH bend then R again for Minton. There, fork R 1.2m to Hamperley X-roads.

R again and at forest edge, fork L through gate onto forest road. A 2m serpentine uphill ride to clear the forest, crest the Mynd, down 200yds and then R (NNE) on the Port Way for 0.4m. L (NW) and down on bridleway to cross Asterton lane (steep. sharp L bend near lane!) onto muddy track N.

2.5m on, it's tarmac now, L at T-junction through Medlicott to Bridges 1.7m away. L by pub, L again then R onto narrow lane. About 0.5m keep L and up into car park, on R, 1.5m further on.

Take track (NNE) 1.1m, to L fork (footpath on map, bridleway on ground) across field to gate. SO (NW) 350yds, to top of Stiperstones Ridge. R (NNE) on track for 0.75m. Fork R, through gate, 250yds, out of another gate onto moor. SO (NE) at first then track swings R(S) to gate (info board 18). Climb vague stile on L. Turn L (NE) and follow derelict wall for 100yds. R on track. This swings R/L on lazy, 400yds 'S' to gate. SO (NE) across field, past house onto track, down through farm (slow! leave gates as found please) and to road; 1m downhill in all.

R for 2m. L (E) onto track to lane, 1.8m away. R (S) for 0.75m. L at T-junction, uphill 1.2m then R (SE) onto Port Way. After 2.5m cross lane.

SO (E) for 0.3m to keep R, away from boundary, onto obvious grassy track for 1m. Gets gritty (speed freaks beware!) before

meeting lane. L then quickly R onto grass, waymarked bridleway, E across Plush Hill (footpath on map). 300yds on do not swing S, keep roughly ENE, down across 'Pony Ring'. Sharp L then R bend (Slow! Walkers!) on obvious single track before meeting lane. R, down to B4370. R and back to town, 2m away.

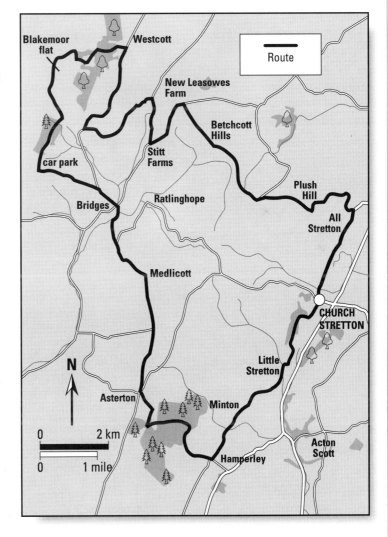

INFO: LONG MYND

BIKE SHOPS

Long Mynd Cycles (Tel: 01694 72367) are staffed by a friendly, MTBing team and they also hire MTBs.

NOTES

The National Trust respectfully ask that mountain bikers keep clear of Carding Mill Valley. It's a real honey-pot for tourists and already suffers from over-use.

zigzagging down to New Leasowes. More tarmac. This time for just a short spin over Stitt Hill and back onto The Port Way for the final assault of the ride. Over the Mynd.

Brendon and Roger had promised a grand finale – a 2 mile descent – so, with renewed vigour, we motored through High Park Hollow, up over the road then dropped four-in-line on some fast-track over the turf. A chip in Cross Dyke's distant bank in our sights.

A long clear run ahead invited a spin. I cranked hard to get my 48-12 combo humming and put some steam down. Roger and Brendon dipped through the Dyke and out of sight while I, intent on picking up their lines, followed on. The speeding duo's every flick, twist and turn read the trail aloud to me – the rest was a blur. I tried to steal a glance at the speedo but the trail tripped down a rocky defile, kicking the bike skyward. Once. Twice. Three times airborne and 'max speed' was not a priority. Nor was landing – I'd already hit the deck sprinting but suddenly the legs stopped dead. It was the damn chain! Jammed! Dropping the back wheel out sorted the problem and we regrouped on the lane at Plush Hill for the final run through the 'Pony Ring' down to Inwood and town. A sweet piece of single track if ever there was one and, when Brendon suggested another run before we made tracks, who could disagree?

MINTON BATCH BASH

Distance: 16 miles. Climb total: 2000ft. Time: 3 hours.

A real leg-stretcher that packs in a couple of serpentine calf-singers but the pay-out is two miles of manic downhill in Minton Batch a tricky ravine with some tasty, technical single tracking.

Carving out a corner on Cotswold cart track near Hailes

R on the X-roads at the W end of Sandford Avenue (GR453938) in Church Stretton. On the B4370 for 1.4m then L up Castle Hill Lane for 1m to Jinlye, Plush Hill. (Alternative off-road route: on B4370 L after 1.2m, just before pub, then fork R after 150yds up track to Castle Hill lane to Jinlye.) Turn L, leave

tarmac behind and head NW for 1m; then swing SW, still on track, for 1.6m past a mound, the Shooting Box, to a lane.

A quick R/L and it's back to moorland track. Down to gate, 1.25m, then on farm track to unclassified tarmac. L, then R at T-

junction. SO for 1m to gated track on L. Up to the Port Way (metalled section), R for 1.3m (just before the Gliding Club) then L (E) onto bridleway single track down into Minton Batch. 2m to lane (tricky bits on upper section!). L to Minton. L to Little Stretton. L, onto B4370, back to town.

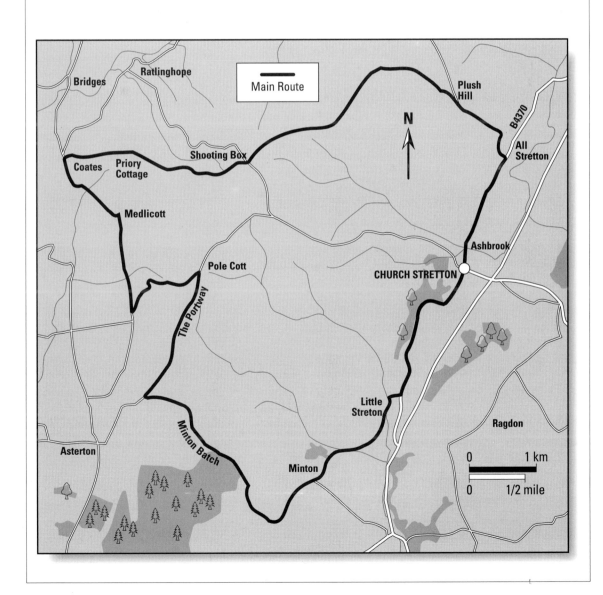

Pennines in Contrast

THE PEAK DISTRICT

If you're looking for isolation close to home, with thrills and spills thrown in, then the Peak ('Peac' is a hill in Old English) National Park, way up on the spine of England, is where it's at. Best known for its dark crags, cliffs and peat plateau, the Park's northern flank features an austere landscape known as the High Peak. Criss-crossed by prehistoric paths, ancient pack-horse tracks and abandoned railways of a bygone era, the High Peak is packed with contours in attractive contortions that'll quicken the pulse of any MTBer, prepared to put their heart where their mouth is. We're talking an MTB stomping ground where shredding the edge is the name of the game! It's rough, tough and craggy. Almost every trail packs a technical challenge and the landscape's stunning. A medley of great gritstone edges, cavernous limestone gorges, grim moorland and green pastureland cut across with miles of dry-stone walling.

Way down in Edale-down-in-the-Dale – a hamlet nestling in the heart of the Peak National Park – it's prime-time MTBing territory that's easy to get to, simple to stay in and impossible to leave. Once you've shredded Rushup Edge, witnessed Whinstone's windswept vistas and jellied your legs traversing Jaggers Clough, you'll know what I mean! And then, further west, there's Whaley Bridge where the dark hills of the High Peak dominate the skyline. Built in dun-coloured stone of sombre mood, Whaley is a bustling community with a proud industrial heritage. A heritage that has furnished it with a network of towpaths and dismantled railways, giving direct access to the surrounding hills and dales of the National Park. Ideal for the likes of us!

RUSHUP ROUND

Distance: 20 miles. Climb total: 3000ft. Time: 3 hours (dry), 4 hours (wet).

A rich mix of Dark and White Peak trail-blazing with some hyper-speed tarmac thrown in. An ideal intro ride for tyro trail-blazers new to the territory.

It was late in the day when we finally managed to kick cranks, speed off down Edale YHA's drive, hopping speed humps and revelling in the awesome valleyscape that surrounded us. Late afternoon sun saw us sauntering along Edale's leafy lane. A light breeze sent the first leaves of fall scuttling across the tarmac and autumnal air, heavy with the scent of reflection, still held sufficient of summer's heat for us to ride short-sleeved.

An exciting ride was in prospect, kicking off with some instant

INFO: EDALE

ACCESS

Edale has a 2-hourly service on the Manchester–Sheffield line (Tel: 0161 832 8353); 50 mins from Manchester Piccadilly and 30 mins from Sheffield. There's a biker-friendly service on week-ends but during the week avoid commuter times and book in advance.

The A625, what's left of it, from the A6 in the west and from Sheffield in the east runs right past Edale, just a stone's throw south. From the west, turn off the A625 at Windy Knoll (just before the Mam Tor car park) or at Hope if you're up from the east.

MAPS

OS Outdoor Leisure 1:25 000 1 The Peak District – Dark Peak (revised 1995 edition); OS 1:50 000 Landranger 110 Sheffield Huddersfield and 119 Buxton, Matlock and Dove Dale; Harveys 1:40 000 Dark Peak North and Dark Peak South.

Contour clipping at Cowburn, at the beginning of The High Peak Trail off-road trek

DIRECTIONS → → → → → 　　　　RUSHUP ROUND

Start Edale car parks (GR125853 GR123853) (security can be a problem – lock your car!). From T-junction, head WSW for 100yds then turn L (ESE) for 0.5m to Greenlands. Turn L (ENE), contouring at first, for 0.75m on bridleway to Hollins Cross.

Turn R (WSW), along ridge, for 0.6m then keep R (WSW), round N side of Mam Tor fort, for 0.5m to road. Turn L (SSW) for 0.1m.

Turn R (WSW) through gate onto bridleway for 1.4m, past Lord's Seat, to go through bridleway gate and continue (SW) for 0.9 miles to A625. Turn R (WSW) for 0.1m to T-junction, turn L (SSE) for 1m, past Whitelee, then turn L (E) for 1m (watch out for quarry lorries –

they're large, fast and lunatic!) to T-junction with bridleway track just past Eldon Hill Quarry.

Fork R (E) (heavy plant bumbling about – take care!) for 0.7m, just past humongous hole, then turn R (S) 25yds, through gate. Continue for 1.25m on bridleway over spur to execute a very lazy R/L to gated track down to T-junction with road.

Turn L (SE) for 200yds to Old Dam X-roads and there fork L (E) for 0.3m. Then turn L (NNE) on bridleway drive for 0.1m to track T-junction. Turn R (ENE) following obvious gated track for 1m, along Oxlow Rake, to bridleway T-junction by a gate. Keep L (N then NNE) for 0.5m to track X-roads N of quarry.

Go SO then swing R (NE) along Limestone Way for 0.25m to path T-junction in valley bottom. Then turn R (E), through metal gate, for 1.25m down Cave Dale to T-junction in Castleton.

Turn L (W) for 0.1m, swinging almost immediately R (N), to T-junction on A625 then turn L (W) for 0.5m (Rose Cottage Café, with its railings, is an ideal pit-stop) to T-junction. Keep R (WNW) for 2m, following old main road (there's an interesting info board at the turning point near Mam Farm) as it zigzags below Mam Tor, to T-junction with A625 and B6061.Turn R (W) for 0.5m to T-junction, turn R (NE) for 0.4m, over Mam Tor col, to pick up outbound bridleway and fork R (NNE) for 1.1m to Hollins Cross. Fork L (N then NE), keeping L of the obvious gully at first, for 1m down bridleway single track, track then farm drive to T-junction. Turn L (W) for 1m to start.

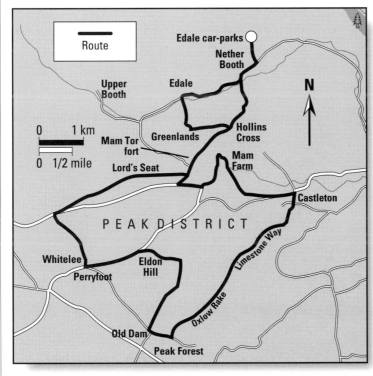

INFO: EDALE

ACCOMMODATION

The best place to stay is Edale YHA and Activity Centre at Rowland Cote (Tel: 01433 670302) (GR140866). Outdoor pursuits is the name of the game here (including MTBing), so a bunch of mad, muddy mountain bikers like your good selves will be made welcome. The nearest, alternative YHA is Castleton (Tel: 01433 620235). Edale is peppered with B&Bs and hotels and Buxton TIO (Tel: 01298 25106) or the Peak National Park Info Centre in Edale (Tel: 01433 620207) have details.

NOTES

It's well worth visiting the National Park Information Centre at Edale – latest weather forecasts are available.

height gain on the track up to Hollins Cross. It's a col with some stupendous, 'sense-u-round' views but, with shadows already lengthening, we had little time to linger. On and up. Down round the ramparts of Mam Tor Fort we were treated to a quick downhill dash on single track that dipped and dived to the road.

We didn't exactly rush up Rushup Edge. It was more of a granny-cog slog up steep, stepped grass single track that was sheer torture for me. I hadn't been out on the bike lately. Rushup was enjoying a respite from its wind-blown reputation and that made for an easy ridge ride before dropping down to a rocky gully, where a notice entreated us to stick to the sunken track. No encouragement needed! Bare rock strata and rubble arranged in a rude flight of steps tricked it out with a technical edge. Not extreme – a case of letting the bike roll and riding with it. Love it!

Out of the gully and straight into a slick, super-quick descent on tarmac that had us sweeping down the fellside at 40-plus. And all in a freewheel! The huge hole in the hill that's Eldon Hill Quarry was a sobering sight and a spectacular monument to our mad obsession with motorway mileage. But saddened spirits were lifted on the far side of the hill, up above Peak Forest, in the light of the sun as it sank towards the far horizon, filling the landscape with gold. Our trail dipped, we slipped in 46-12, spun the SPUDs and rode in spiritual mode down the trail to Old Dam. Talk about an after-glow!

Now we were in limestone land, snaking our way along Cave Dale on slick-rock single track; slip-sliding down paths of oolitic ooze that clogged tyres and sent the bikes into a crab-wise slither. Odd how this dale is home to more species of slug than any other spot in England.

Beyond Castleton we took on the shattered chicanes of the old A625. Massive multi-layer tarmac slabs, buckled, tossed and cracked, surrounded us. All very 'after the bomb'; we felt like sole survivors. Then we were back on track, sweet single track, for the heady ridge ride down to Hollins Cross. With the sun now set we really were sole survivors so we spun pedals and enjoyed the rare delights of jamming down this track at speed. But our day in the Peaks was far from done and, as the path tripped off the ridge, we hooked up on a superb section of sinuous single track that dropped us down to Edale wide-eyed and hungry for more.

RESERVOIR AND RUSHUP TURN

Distance: 32 miles. Climb total: 3400ft. Time: 5 hours (dry), 8 hours (wet).

It's tortuous, it's tough, it's technical. Four interlinked loops if you've got the time, one or two singles if you don't.

Kinder's towering edges cut the northern horizon, enclosing Edale's homely vale with a rolling rampart of clough and spur. Awesome. We were climbing the track to Wooler Knoll, already warmed up on a spin down the dale on tarmac and ready for something a bit radical. We got it sure enough. Switchback track, boulder-strewn and seriously steep winds down into Woodlands Valley. Chris – my trailmate for the day – was in his element; executing track-stands, picking lines, finessing his way through on instinct and focus that are the mark of a fine rider. I followed, dabbed and scrabbled a few times and learnt a lot about balance.

With little let-up in the roller-coaster regime it was straight back into more steep switchbacks. Up Hagg Side. This is heaven for hill climbers who get ecstatic when the trail feeds them with a constant trickle of tasty technical teasers. Exhausted from fighting gravity, we loosened up on the long descent past Crookhill Farm.

Local riders had raved on about how brilliant a detour round Whinstone Lee Tor would be and they were right. It encapsulates the essence of Peak trail-blazing; capricious climbs, ruts, bumps, big air-time, dipping and diving down the radical descent to the Derwent Valley with prime-time views to greet the eye if you can tear your gaze away from the gritty track ahead! Enter euphoria.

The most picturesque off-road river crossing in England? The Wye in the White Peak

High-tailing it into Edale from Hollins Cross in the heart of the National Park (below)

By comparison the fast-track run-down past Rowlee Farm was pretty tame, though the chicanes spiced it up, slipped in a tyre skip or two and pepped up the pulse rate.

We hit the rubbly bridleway up Blackey Hey late in the day. This looked like it would have to be the last big climb of our loop. Random rubble and rutted cart track not only tested traction, but the ping-pong effect had us zigzagging crazily in an effort to stay on course. Chris rose to the challenge, stormed up the hill to leave me scrabbling and dabbing in a vain effort to reel him in. Jaggers Clough sounded extreme and sure enough it was. A couple of steps cut the chat, gave the adrenalin factor a kick as we dropped into the clough for one legendary descent. Despite fatigue it was instant off-road ecstasy. Drops, dips, water runnels running all over, bedrock steps with a sprinkling of stones to add the essential

D I R E C T I O N S → → → → →

Start Edale car parks (GR125853 GR123853) (lock your car!) and, from T-junction, head (E) for 4m, past YHA then back under railway again. Pick up county unclassified road off L (NNE) just before bridge over River Noe.

Climb for 2.4m, past farm entrance and on to join gated track, to bridleway.X-roads just beyond Hope Cross. Then turn R for 1m, down through steep R/L/R/L zigzags (boulder-strewn – beware!) in forest, over bridge and on up to A57.

Zigzag L/R (effectively SO) 100yds up Hagg Farm drive then keep R (N) up switchback bridleway track for 0.4m to bridleway X-roads. Turn R (SE) for 1.5m, SO at bridleway T-junction and over Bridge-end Pasture, to field gate after grass descent. Swing L (ESE then SSE) for 1m, following guide posts to track, to pick up Crookhill Farm drive down to road.

Turn R (S) for 0.5m to A57 then turn L for 0.25m, over bridge. Fork L (E) up tarmac bridleway at first for 0.25 miles, through Ashopton, to join single track after 2nd gate. SO (E) for 1.5m on roller-coaster bridleway, crossing rocky ford, to lip of Highshaw Clough.

Here bridleway swings L (N then W) to climb for 1 mile to col at Whinstone Lee Tor (viewpoint!). Then swing R (N) for 0.75m on contouring bridleway to T-junction. Then turn L (W) for 0.9m on obvious single track (steep and/or rubbly at times), between two barns, down to gated track.

Turn R (NW) alongside Ladybower Reservoir for 1.5m, joining tarmac, crossing valley to T-junction by Information Centre car park. (Eats kiosk here. WCs only in winter.) Turn R (NNE) for 1.25m, along (W) side of Derwent Reservoir. Fork L (SSW then SE) for 1.5m, up through forest then past Lockerbrook Farm, to familiar

bridleway X-roads above Hagg Farm.

Fork R (WSW then NW) for 1m, on obvious track that turns to switchback tarmac road, past Rowlee Farm to A57. Go SO (SW) for 0.4m to bridleway T-junction then turn L (ESE) to climb for 1.5 miles, over ford, to familiar bridleway X-roads near Hope Cross.

Turn R (SW) for 1.5m, through Jaggers Clough (steep, rutted descent!) on obvious track passing (N) of Clough Farm, to outbound road. Turn R (SW) for 2.6m, passing through Edale and over River Noe, to pick up gated bridleway track off R (SW).

Climb for 1.5m up Chapel Gate Track (seriously steep in places), swinging L (S) over spur, to bridleway T-junction. Turn L (E then ENE) for 0.5 miles to bridleway gate (easy to miss).

technical edge. All topped off with a water splash. We were still
buzzing from making the drop with barely a dab between us
when, all of sudden, we were back on that leafy lane in the bosom
of Edale.

HIGH PEAK, OFF-PEAK

Distance: 30 miles. Climb total: 4000ft. Time: 5 hours (dry),
6.5 hours (wet).

High-tail it into the hills on a roller-coaster route that demands
peak performance.

With my propensity for picking the right place but the wrong time
to perfection, I was pounding the High Peak trails in the company
of Stuart Gascoigne – Open Country's owner – in the wake of the

RESERVOIR AND RUSHUP TURN

Swing R and go through gate then
continue (ENE) beside wall for
1.4m along Rushup Edge to road.
L (N) 200yds to pick up gated

bridleway off R (NNE) for 1.1m to
Hollins Cross. Fork L (N then NE),
keeping L of the obvious gully at
first, for 1m down bridleway

single-track, track then farm drive
to T-junction. Turn L (W) for 1m to
start.

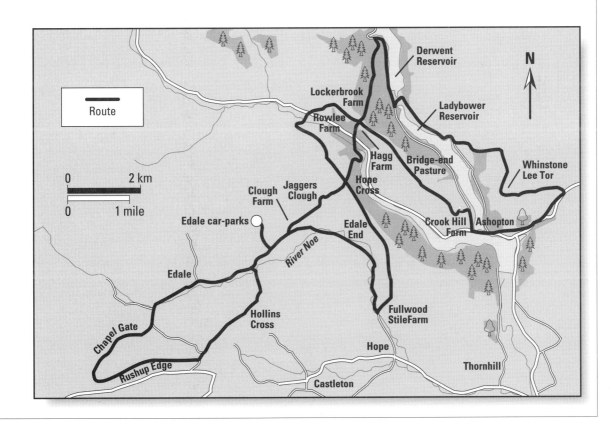

INFO: WILD PEAKS OF WHALEY

ACCESS

BR (Tel: 0161 832 8353) run an hourly Sprinter train between Manchester and Buxton via Whaley Bridge with the usual limited bike-carrying capacity. The Manchester-Sheffield Inter-City service stops at Chinley, just a couple of miles from Whaley.

By road from the M6, exit at J17 and head east via Macclesfield on the A534/A536/ A5002 route; from the M63 J12 head south on the A6; from the M1 use J29 and head west on the A617/A619/A623 trans-Peak road.

MAPS

OS 1:25 000 Outdoor Leisure Maps, 1 the Dark Peak.

ACCOMMODATION

Ringstones Farm campsite, Yeardsley Lane in Furness Vale (Tel: 01663 732152) is the budget option. There are no YHAs in Whaley, but a privately owned alternative is Burnage Hostel (Tel: 0161 432 1527) which sleeps 23. For B&Bs, hotels etc. try the Buxton TIO (Tel: 01298 25106) or the Macclesfield TIO (Tel: 01625 504114).

worst blizzards for years! Slush, slime and sodden single track sans traction were an ever-present and unusual – I was assured – distraction.

By the time we'd reached the Roych track we'd already encountered mud, flood, slime and slush and that was the easy bit! On the Roych the real off-roading started with a ice-packed, rut and rubble descent to the Roych ford, where a trio of lads on Motor Cross bikes were busily chewing and spewing up rocks on the stepped climb-out. Time for a short detour.

Though the day was drab and the sky a doom-laden grey, nothing could dispel the awe at the spectacular scenery that unfolded around us. Even trudging across the tundra that was Tom Moor didn't dampen spirits and by the time we reached Rushup Edge, Stuart was waxing mellifluent on the merits of his moors. With a crisp, ear-clipping wind whisking over the ridge and the incessant slurps from fat tyres spurting water, this was winter riding in extremis. Nothing for it but to hallucinate some heat, sun and skylarks and enjoy the High Peak's most impressive ridge ride, through rose-tinted glasses.

Rushup ended in a quagmire. Tyres blew up big and brown. Grip slipped away and we performed a slow-motion, dual slalom slide down the slope. Spooky! Back on tarmac we took on speed, mud flew and the rubber reappeared in a reassuring black and knobbly sort of way. But the brake pads didn't. Stuart's had all but vanished; so fast that you'd expect to have seen a dark-grey line stretch back across the landscape. So Stuart blagged my spare ones, and just as well, because the drop off Hollins Cross was steep and scary enough with the slush and slime, let alone without brakes!

Time was against us so the programmed tea-stop in Edale was deleted and we pushed up the pace for the short road ride to Lee Farm. Looming ahead in dramatic folds, the fellsides of Kinder Scout hid Jacob's Ladder, the Peak's most celebrated climb. It kicks off with a lung-busting zigzag up a 1:2 hillside and this calf-killer continues for almost a mile to Edale Cross. It's a test for the terminally fit – today ice sheets, mire and a motivation dump had us pushing from the first bend! Looking back, it's one hell of a descent. An eyeballs out, eminently stackable exit off Kinder!

Snow was thawing fast, revealing hidden tracks and making riding a whole lot easier. Fun too with all that run-off rushing down waterlogged trails. Down by Kinder Reservoir snow-melt had gouged out steps and runnels on a precipitous plunge to the service road. I wiped out with finesse. Ahead, Stuart on his full-suspension steed sailed serenely over ditch and drop-off, oblivious to my downfall!

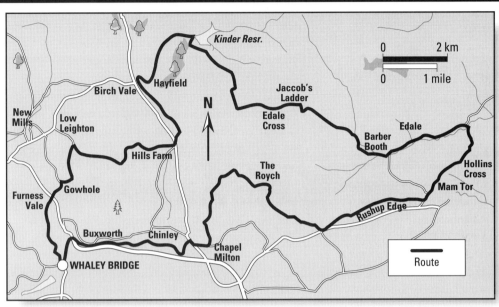

Start from Open Country (GR 012814). L (N) for 200yds then R (NE) down to towpath on E side of Peak Forest Canal basin. L (N) 0.4m, cross footbridge then R (E), over River Goyt, under A6 for 0.5m on N side of canal to Navigation Inn. Go SO (E) road and continue on track for 2m, through industrial estates, SO two roads, past sewage works to road.

L (NNE) 0.4m to A624, then R (SSE) for 0.2m and L (E) for 0.25m towards Wash. L (N) for 0.5m then R (ENE) up lane then track for 1.4m to Roych track. R (SE) for 2.5m, over Roych ford and on to A625.

L (ENE) then L (NE) after 0.1m onto bridleway track by wall for 0.8m. Go through then continue (NE) beside wall for 1.4m along Rushup Edge to road. L (N) 150yds to take bridleway off R that contours Mam Tor then onto

ridge to Hollins Cross 1.1m away.

L (NNE not WNW) 1m to road. L (W) up Edale, past café, 1.75m to T-junction at Barber Booth. R (W) beneath railway on lane then track for 2m to cross footbridge below Jacob's Ladder. Keep L (SSW) and continue for 1.75m up through gate, past Edale Cross to T-junction with single track bridleway off R.

Turn R (N) for 0.4m to gate. SO (N) for 0.3m, round corner of wall, onto track to gate. Go L (WNW). After 0.4m trail veers R (NNW) 0.2m to wood. L (WNW) 0.4m, over track X-roads, down steep descent to Kinder Reservoir service road. Fork R (NNE) up paved bridleway for 0.2m then L (NW) just before steps for 0.3m up to Snake Path signpost.

L (WSW not NW) on Snake Path, through several field gates, 1.3m

to road. R (NW) 0.2m into Hayfield then keeping L (to head S) 0.1m past 'Twenty Trees Café' (good R&R stop). Fork L/R (SSE) up Highgate Road to Roych track 1m from Snake Path exit. Opposite barn fork L (SSE) on track 0.5m then R (SW) 0.2m to A624.

L (S) 130yds then R (W) 100yds on lane then SO (W) on track for 1m, round Hills Farm to T-junction at Chinley Churn track. L (S) 0.4m to T-junction by post then R (WNW) 0.8m SO (WNW) X-roads for 0.5m to go L (SW) by Brownhill Farm.

R (WSW) after 0.75m for 0.7m, through sharp L bend at Gowhole, to A6. Busy road take care! SO (SW) staggered R/L X-roads 0.4m to fork L just past Yeardsley Hall. Keep L (SSW) after 0.25m. 0.4m to Hockerley, keeping L (SSE) after stream. R (S) 0.4m, over X-roads in estate, to T-junction. L (E) 0.3m down into Whaley.

Over Snake Path – an ancient trans-Dark Peak route – and down to Hayfield we took the clearer trails at speed. I clicked in the top cog for the first time and heard the slipstream sing in the skid-lid straps. Great! The warm lights of the Twenty Trees Café hove into view, I smelt hot tea cakes but Stuart motored on up Highgate Road. Damn! Tiring limbs, weary of the endless struggle for traction, still managed to keep the cranks turning for what was a cruel climb over Chinley Churn and, with dusk hard on our heels, we hurtled down to Gowhole on a demonic, ice-covered descent. Hot showers and supper beckoned, the drizzle deterred, so we opted out of the little loop round Ringstones, and raced for home.

INFO: WILD PEAKS OF WHALEY

BIKE SHOPS

Open Country (Tel: 01663 735020) is *the* bike shop in the area. The staff are keen MTBers and they have a well-equipped workshop. Plus they have all the maps, mags, hire off-road machines and you can step next door for a bun 'n' brew in their bikers' café, swap trail tales and have a good time without getting wet and muddy.

HAYFIELD HOP

Distance: 20 miles. Climb total: 2600ft. Time: 2.5hours.

Cruise above the creeping conurbation on a double loop with pub 'n' café stops a plenty. This is the ideal, not-too-technical taster when tourists are chock-a-block along the better-known trails.

Boulder-strewn steps characterise the tricky drop down the Roych Clough (above)

The switch-back track on the infamous Jacob's Ladder – a leg-killer of a climb; demonic in descent (right)

Start from Open Country (GR 012814). L (N) for 200yds then R (NE) down to towpath on E side of Peak Forest Canal basin. L (N) 0.4m, cross footbridge then R (E), over River Goyt, under A6 for 0.5m on N side of canal.

L (NE) on road by Navigation Inn, SO (NE) at T-junction, under railway to T-junction 0.5m away. L (NNW) for 0.4m then R (NE) at T-junction for 0.5m. R (ESE) below Chinley Churn for 200yds to track off L (NNW).

Follow track for 1.2m then bear L (N) down to gate 0.9m away. SO (NW) down lane 0.5m to A6015. L (WSW) then immediately R (W) for 0.25m. R (ENE) up paved track 0.5m to road for a quick R then L (NNE) back on track for 1m, through gate, down to junction by Blackshaw Farm.

SO (NNW) for 0.75m, past Matleymoor Farm and through gate, to single-track bridleway off R (N). Follow bridleway across moor 0.25m to bend on road. SO (N) on road 0.3m then L (W) on farm road. Keep R (W) onto track after 0.4m, over Cown Edge, L/R round dog-leg, past Robin Hood's Picking Rods for 1.25m to road.

L (SE) on road 1.25m to T-junction. L (ESE) 1m, past pub at Rowarth, to fork R (SE) by Laneside Farm and onto track for 1.25m to road. L (ENE) for 0.25m then sharp R (SW) down outbound track 0.5m to road.

L (E) 0.25m to A6015 then R (SW) for 0.2m, past chapel, to fork L (SW) onto unclassified road that turns to track. After 2.3m meet outbound road below Chinley Churn. Keep R (SW) for 2.5m to return to Whaley on outbound route.

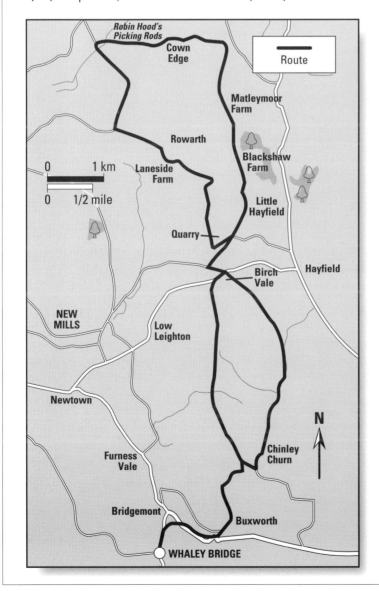

CHAPTER SIX

Riding Riggs

NORTH YORK MOORS

The North York Moors are the most spectacular splash of purple in England. Visit them when summer's giving a last blast before sinking into autumn, and you'll be treated to a mass of mauve so rich that even Ringle trick bits pale in comparison. Spectacular as it is, purpleness isn't the main attraction for off-road fanatics – prime-time MTBing is!

Sinuous single track. Pale trails cutting serpentine lines through a deep sea of heather. So florific and full of fragrance that it makes you giddy! But there's no time for fuzzy heads. Bar the bracken – which can stand 10 feet tall – and the mud – when Nature turns on the taps, perfect trails pack in everything from amicable cruising to shredding the edge, as in when fear/ecstasy become inextricably mixed. It's eyes down, skipping rocks and hopping ruts on a plethora of technical tracks that make these moors the MTB nirvana of the North.

But, despite the obvious delights of kicking dirt up here – where offshore breezes, sun, a sea of heather and a good dose of hammertime prove a heady mix – nobody seems to know they exist. After days of trail-bashing there, our tyre tracks were the only witness.

INFO: NORTH YORK MOORS

ACCESS

The best rail route is via the Middlesborough /Whitby line which have two bikes per trip locos and it's a case of turn up and hope. The York/Scarborough line is much the same. BR info (Tel: 0912 326262) have the details. By road from the south take the A64 off the A1 then the A169. From the north the A171 via Middlesborough's the best way in.

FLYING ABOVE FYLINGDALES

Distance: 21 miles. Climb total: 2000ft. Time: 2.5 hours (dry), 4 hours (wet).

Double loop to hone trail skills on some delectable dirt track through heath and heather.

We'd barely clicked into the ride routine when we barrelled into

DIRECTIONS → → → → →

Start Boggle Hole car park (GR952037). Go (SSW and away from the Bay) 0.6m on lane to turn L (SSW) on single track bridleway for 0.6m, across stream then on zigzag climb up valley side, to Scarborough–Whitby railpath.

Turn R (WSW) for 0.9m to junction with C road then turn L (W) 250yds to T-junction. Then L (W) 1m, through Swallow Head Farm onto bridleway track, to bridleway T-junction in field corner. L (W) 0.9m, joining St Ives Farm track, to A171. R (NNW) 1m then L (WNW) on B1416 1.8m to X-roads, then 2nd L (SW) 0.9m to join track by car park.

SO (S at first) 0.75m, past Foss Farm, then R (NW) at T-junction, 0.3m to go through Leas Head Farm. 100yds beyond yard L (NW) across field to gate. L (NW, S then W) 0.8m on track to moor gate. SO (SW) 0.75m on roughly contouring path to ford. SO (SW) 0.5m up to Whinstone Ridge track (next 3m can get seriously muddy). L (ESE) 1.25m to York Cross bridleway signpost, keep R (S then SSE) 2m to Louven Howe Rig.

Swing L (ESE) 250yds to bridleway X-roads then L (NE, Robin Hood's Bay) 2m to post (marked 9) on track. Swing R (NE) 250yds on track, fork R (NNE) 0.7m over heather (local riders say there's a path, NYMNP rangers say not), to small isolated pine tree by path, then swing R (ENE) 0.5m to ravine. R (SSE) 350yds to gate.

SO (SE) 100yds to A171, R (ESE) 0.3m to St Ives Farm track then L (ENE) 0.5m to bridleway T-junction. L (NNE) 0.6m to Ramsdale Mill, hairpin L (W) 0.8m, over river, to T-junction. Keep R (NE) 0.3m to Fyling Hall. On road L (N) 300yds, R (NE) 100yds to T-junction then SO (NNE) 0.9m, through Fylingthorpe, to X-roads with railpath on bends. R (SSW) 0.75m on path to crossing, then L (SSE) 0.5m, through Mill Beck ford and farm, to start.

Stoupe Beck's short 'n' sweet chute down to the river and our ideas of a summer's sojourn by the sea were blown clean away! Something had been missing from rides of late, and sensuous single track was it. Time to embrace excitement and anticipate the exhilaration of an afternoon's off-roading!

Across the valley our crudely paved cart track connected with the Scarborough–Whitby railpath, at a point suddenly familiar to Aaron and I. It was here, near the close of the first MTB coast-to-coast ride, that we'd paused for breath before the final dash down to Robin Hood's Bay. The dark track and dappled light dislodged a myriad of memories for us, and Aaron said it was just like coming home – in a funny sort of way.

Out onto the open brow of Swallow Head Hill we had an ocean to our backs, billowing heather moor ahead and the fertile fragrance of sea and fern filling our lungs. But before the moor we had some tarmac to tone up on, with a fine off-road descent down past Falling Foss Falls (it's a popular beauty spot so beware of walkers), followed by a roller-coaster ride up the valley and out onto open heath. The North Yorkshire Moors are famous for fun-time, semi-technical single track ('techno-track' in jargonese.) The sort to tease your skills, put pep in the pedals and get a bit of off-road rhythm going. Our piece of path started innocently enough in

Foster Howes. Dry like this and it's dusty. When it's sodden it's a slog in a bog

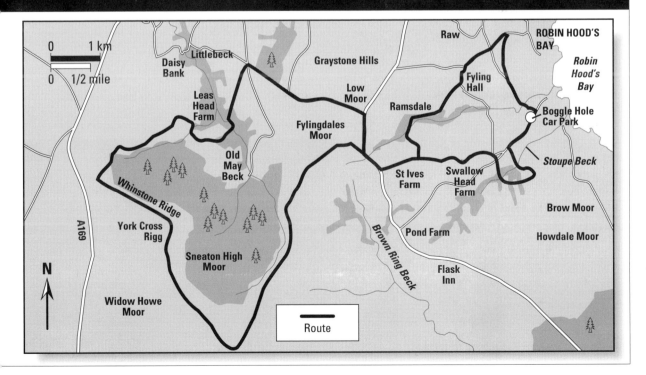

FLYING ABOVE FYLINGDALES

INFO: NORTH YORK MOORS

MAPS

OS 1:25000 Outdoor Leisure Maps 26 NYM – West and 27 NYM – East; OS 1"/mile Touring Map Guide The North York Moors; OS 1:50000 Landranger 94 Whitby.

BIKE SHOPS

There's a bike shop in Whitby and more in Scarborough but locals recommend Richardson's Cycles (Tel: 0723 352682) in Scarborough's Castle Road, where they are keen off-roaders.

ACCOMMODATION

Boggle Hole YHA (Tel: 0947 88035) is on the seashore in Robin Hood's Bay and there's Wheeldale YHA (Tel: 0947 86350) located in the heart of the moors, but if you prefer private accommodation or a camp-site, ring Whitby TIO (Tel: 0947 602674) or the North Yorkshire Moors National Park (Tel: 0723 372351) for info.

a rough, lawn-like way but as we gained height and hit the heather, random rocks kicked up the technical quotient and had us skipping and weaving in delight. Things took a radical turn on the dip through the rubble-strewn gully of Flass Brow – dab-dab time – before the trail cut a rut – or three – through the purple swathe.

Back to track. Broad and rough with a dash of the downhill element to entice the tyres to spin, it was an ideal opener for what was in store off the top of Louven Howe. Robin Hood's Bay Road (path) was the venue, off-road ecstasy the name of the game. Over a mile of prime-time techno-trail, with rocks to hop, ruts to rip, steps to skip and a crazy rhythm that entreats the unwary to take it to the radical. Trouble is that this truly sensuous piece of single track simply disappears into the blue, after it departs the track on Shooting House Rigg. Undeterred, we took a bearing, headed across the heather and finally touched on intermittent trail by a pygmy pine tree. The trail went full-time on the lip of a ravine – and nearly enticed us to take an impromptu dive – and we made the main road with relief. I am glad it wasn't foggy!

A brief blast down the drive to St Ives Farm reminded us that the exceptional is not restricted to moorland riggs (take care when you drop in – the track passes through the yard). Cart tracks here-abouts are quite capable of springing some unexpected tyre skip and giving the heart rate a kick, as one of us found when we hit the hairpin at Ramsdale Mill a bit too hard. Lucky there was room for an overshoot!

Dusk was upon us for the final off-road dash down to Fyling Hall. From there we took in some tortuous tarmac, a cruise along cindered railpath and a surprise plummet down to and into Mill Beck before we breasted the hill above Boggle Hole. A real granny grinder, so save something for this last grapple with gravity.

Little did we know it but Robin Hood Bay Road was about to disappear into the heather

GLAISDALE GALLOP

Distance: 27 miles. Climb total: 3500ft. Time: 5 hours (dry),
7.5 hours (wet).

Too short by far. Sumptuous scenery featuring the best single
track this side of the North Sea.

Local MTB hero Pete Tomkins had waxed lyrical on a legendary
loop out of Lealholm, so I felt duty bound to take a look. It was a
cracking day – crystal-clear air, azure sky and just a kiss of wind
to cool off the climbs. Our track ran right out of the car park for a
roller-coaster run alongside the river. Anticipation of a great day's
trail-shredding had us prancing about like a group of gazelles on
new grass. All this cocky exuberance was bound to catch us out. It
did. Beyond Park House Farm we flew down the track, caught
some speed-given fly-time off the rail bridge flat, hit the bend at
the bottom a touch too hard and hurtled headlong into a huge puddle! Wet, wet, wet! Be warned friends, it's almost always there.

**Spitting grit on empty track along
Glaisdale Rigg**

Pete hadn't warned us about the watery trap, but he had men-
tioned a severe climb-out on the other side of the Esk. Severe is
about the size of it but if you hit the first bend humming then
you're home free. Take it timidly and you can count on a dab or
dismount. Either way, height gain is rapid, the river was quickly
left behind and we were soon up on the riggs where the air was
fresh and the views stunning. On this loop there's little let-up on
the roller-coaster theme, and we'd barely paused for breath when
the bridleway grabbed a gully and dropped down into Glaisdale.
There we hummed across the valley on a unique piece of cement
twin-track, courtesy of the local landowner, before getting stuck
into a real granny-cog slog up onto Egton Moor. But all that lactic
leg pain and lung-bursting effort were rewarded by a sweet section
of single track. We strung out and spun cranks, eyes down and
oblivious to the road ahead, until tarmac suddenly turned up under
the tyres!

The road ride round the head of Glaisdale provided a brief
respite from the rough stuff. We cruised along three abreast – cars
are few and far between – and admired the awesome view over the
dales and out to sea. On the lip of Great Fryup Dale – surely
named after a gut-busting breakfast – we switched back into off-
road mode on a bridleway that Pete described in one word:
'Bliss!'. You'd better believe it.

Twisting in and out of the heather, it's a rock-hopping, sinuous
ridge ride where concentration is the key to survival and a silly
grin the reward. We were so enthralled that we careered past the
cairn that marked our drop down into the dale. And it's an impressive pile of rocks!

The by-ways down by the Bay sport some superb single-track

Impressive too is the precipitous path down into the dale. It's a real cliffhanger. Technical in the extreme – with switchbacks, steps and scree to spice up the extra air over the edge – it's a run that's fun for the fearless, ideal for the insane, but the top notch proved a tad beyond our technical expertise. Even down in the dale the trail starts with enough rough stuff to give it a technical edge that demands total concentration. Brilliant! Then there's a dip 'n' dive run down to Raven Hill Farm. Mind the gates!

We'd viewed the exit from Fryup from the far side. It looked like we'd be facing a frantic scramble to Danby Rigg, on a zigzag track that clawed its way up a ragged rock face. In reality it proved to be no more than a path. A rocky, bracken blocked one at that! But, even with the bracken gone, I reckon it's a carry. It was boulders with a capital 'B'! More bar-grabbing bracken made a mockery of what would have been a ridge-top blast down to Botton Farm, so my advice is to skip this dip during late summer. Disenchanted with the descent, we emerged into the fields above the farm with egos dented and a desire for recompense. A steep sweep of grass led to the gate at the bottom so it was time to kick cranks and spin out at max speed. Suddenly the turf opened up, a yawning gap, a step, a track! A track? Desperate anti-stack manoeuvres and I made it. Just! My companions, in close pursuit, couldn't figure out where I'd vanished. Next thing they were airborne, skipped a date with ground-zero, regained control and slewed to a stop, wide-eyed and wondering where in the heck that hole had come from!

Botton's Bakery was closed but luckily we spotted the 'choc ices' sign at East Cliff Farm. Heaven sent, those ices sure hit the spot. Mind you we needed the boost. The climb back up onto Danby Rigg is a killer, which kicks off on grass then hooks up on a switchback track with a calf-grinding gradient. There was no obvious route out onto the rigg so we cut across to some cairns, capped them with a rock in the traditional manner, took a quick dip into Little Fryup Dale, before a setting sun and the onset of dusk saw us back atop Danby Rigg more than ready for the run down to the village. Bliss! The sinking sun spread a golden glow across moorlands awash with mauve, our lengthening shadows rippled over the heather and the Esk, winding down its deep green dale, glittered below. Crash! A rock rammed the front wheel, I was whipped out of my evening reverie, back to track with a technical edge and my two companions careering off into the distance. Time to kick up some serious speed. And with speed came rhythm. A rhythm that melds man and machine, makes every line a winner; rocks and ruts barely touched the treads in a downhill treat, that had all three of us on a high that lasted all the way back to Lealholm. Ever been asked whether the earth moved?

DIRECTIONS → → → → →   GLAISDALE GALLOP

Start Lealholm car park (GR764076). At bottom of car park L (ESE) 0.7m to Underpark Farm. L (N) under bridge then R (ENE) 0.5m to track T-junction. R (ESE) 1m, through Park House Farm, over Esk footbridge and up to T-junction in Glaisdale.

SO (SSW) 0.8m to fork L (WSW) just after pond and drop 0.75m, SO (SW) bridleway X-roads, onto Dale road. R (W) 0.25m then L (SE) 0.5m, through farm to T-junction with path. Keep L (S) 75yds to gate, SO (S), keeping to fence on your R, 0.4m to road at Low Gill Beck Farm. R (WSW) 1m then L (ESE) on Mountain Ash bridleway 0.25m to forest edge. Then turn R (S then SSE) 1m, through gate onto moor, to C road.

R (WSW) 1m to T-junction, R (NNW) 2.1m to bridleway/road X-roads. Take 1st obvious L (SW) Trough House bridleway 1.25m to cairn then R (N) 0.25m (care! drop starts suddenly) to ford. SO (ENE) then swing up R (N) then down and L (E) 0.2m to next ford. SO (N) up to gate then alongside field boundary to gate 0.8m away. R (NE) through gate 0.4m by Raven Hill Farm to road. L (N) 0.6m to T-junction, L (SW) 1m, through Woodhead Farm and RH of twin gates, to gate below ruined barn.

R (WNW), past barn, 0.3m up zigzag path to top gate. Swing R (NW) 0.2m, past grouse butt, to road. SO (NW then N) 0.25m then fork L (NW) on lesser path SO (NW) edge 0.5m to signposted gate. L (W) through gate 0.5m, through Botton Farm (café and bakery open on weekdays) to road T-junction. R (NNE) 0.25m then R (E) 0.2m, round behind East Cliff Farm 0.4m to moor gate.

Climb 250yds up L/R zigzag to top then SO (NE) away from edge, 250yds over heather to Jack Sledge Road path cairns. SO (NE) 0.6m over Danby Rigg to road in Little Fryup Dale, L (ENE) 250yds to X-roads. Fork L (N) on bridleway path 1m, back over Danby Rigg, to moor gate. SO (NNW) 250yds to road, L (NW) 0.6m and then keeping R to T-junction then R (ENE) 0.5m over river to Danby X-roads.

R (E) 275yds, past PO, to bridleway. L (NW) then R (NE) for 200yds up to gate. SO (NE) 200yds up track to wall corner; swing L (NNE) 0.8m to road then R (N) 200yds to bridleway track. R (E) 0.4m to stream. Track swings R (S) but vague bridleway continues (SE) 0.4m to rejoin track. Keep L (SE) 0.75m to road X-roads, L (ENE) 0.75m up to Beacon Hill viewpoint then R (E) 1m to T-junction, R (S) again 0.3m to road. L (SSE) 0.3m to T-junction then R (S) 0.5m down to start.

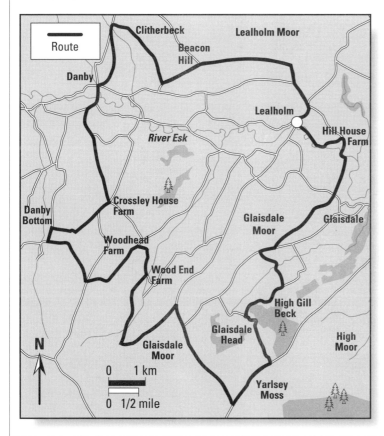

CHAPTER SEVEN

The Barn-Dotted Dales

THE YORKSHIRE DALES

Put me down on a gnarly track, in good company, smack amid spectacular scenery that's bathed in golden light and I'm in heaven! And, pick one spot to come within a slick's skid of being heaven on England's green earth and I'd be in the Yorkshire Dales. Yorkshiremen reckon it's 'God's country'; maybe they're right and, if so, I reckon God rode a mountain bike!

The alien landscape of the limestone pavement hides some of our rarest flora and fauna

Our routes – in the far north and the extreme south of the Yorkshire Dales National Park – encounter radically different types of terrain. On the Park's northern flank, the head of the River Swale is way up among the highest peaks of the Pennine range. Desolate, remote, often hidden in swirling cloud, this barren setting is in cold contrast to the magical valley below Keld. For me, bleak memories of a cold, wet and pain-ridden Polaris Challenge held here are mixed with day rides of brilliant trail-blazing and spinning along the Dale, following *Wheelwright's Coast-to-Coast* route. So what memories endure now? Idyllic, summer's eventide rides above pasture-patterned valleys? Sun warm on the back, a scent of fresh-mown hay on the breeze? Slaking a rare thirst at the Farmer's Arms down in Muker? Or hurtling over spoil heaps in the Hushes? Blasting down drop-offs from Fell End? The lung-busting climb over Kisdon Heights? Well, Swaledale is all of it and it's great.

In the south of the National Park, Malham lies cradled in the dramatic limestone crags of the Craven District. A modest cluster of dale-stone cottages, farmsteads and inns centred upon an ancient packhorse bridge; remote Malham would have remained so, but for the spectacular scenery that surrounds it. Malham Cove,

Upping the grin factor with a Reeth Moor splash 'n' dash routine

INFO: SWALEDALE

ACCESS

Reeth is a favourite weekend base and ideal for us. Built from local, honey-grey sandstone the fine Georgian houses and coaching inns face onto an open green. The nearest BR stations are Darlington and Northallerton 25 miles from Reeth and an easy ride for seasoned saddle polishers.

By motor from the north it's either the M6, A685 Kirkby Stephen, B6270 to Reeth or the A1 Scotch Corner, A6108 Richmond, A6108 then B6270 to Reeth. From the south it's the A1 Leeming, A684 Leyburn, minor road Grinton, B6270 to Reeth and from the west A684 Sedburgh to Bainbridge, minor roads to Askrigg then Swaledale and B6270 to Reeth.

an awesome 250ft limestone wall, brings the valley to an abrupt end just a mile upstream from the bridge. Beyond its curved rim are acres of limestone pavement, stripped of soil by eons of erosion to expose the bedrock. Here you can stumble across the very bones of the earth in an eerie landscape, where dark crevasses split otherwise flat expanses of slick white rock. It's a surrealist setting! Beyond the Cove lies Malham Tarn – a lake in miniature beset by bleak moorland and craggy white cliffs, the shallow waters reflect the mobile mood of the Pennine weather. Janet's Foss and Gordale Scar – a mile or so to the east – are falls where the Gordale Beck negotiates the craggy canyon of the Scar. It's all amazing scenery to be biking in.

REETH MOOR ROUND

Distance: 22 miles. Climb total: 2800ft. Time: 3.5 hours (dry), 4.5 hours (wet).

Scoot round the old mining tracks of Marrick and Reeth, plus a jaunt across the lunar landscape that's the Melbeck Moors. All that adrenalin-inducing trail-blazing finishes off with a heady mix of techno-track and scenic sauntering down the dale home.

SWALEDALE SAUNTER

Distance: 31 miles. Climb total: 3500ft. Time: 5 hours (dry), 7 hours (wet).

A roller-coaster route over the heights of Kisdon and Whitaside, with some prime-time gnarly bits for kicks.

INFO: SWALEDALE

MAPS

OS 1:25 000 Outdoor Leisure 30 Yorkshire Dales – Northern and Central.

ACCOMMODATION

Reeth is chock-a-block with hotels and inns. Book through a Yorkshire Dales National Park Office: Hawes (Tel: 01969 667450) or Aysgarth Falls (Tel: 01969 663424). Grinton YHA (Tel: 01748 84206) or the Punchbowl Inn (Tel: 01748 86233) at Feetham offer budget accommodation.

Barn-dotted Swaledale is one man-made landscape that is beautiful to behold

The first leg, up to Grinton's cattle grid, proved painful to protesting calf muscles. Sweat stung my eyes as my brother Pete and I struggled up the tarmac ribbon. Heather shimmered purple in an early morning heat haze. Suddenly it's summer. A few hundred yards up the hill, a track that heads south-west is available for those keen to take up an off-road alternative. But, in this warmth, we kept on the road and saved our energy.

At last the road levels off and we're pleased to have found the climb much easier than anticipated. There's a sign for the bridleway over Height of Greets but there's no sign of the bridleway. Luckily there is an obvious track a few yards further on. This wends its way through spoil tips, alongside the heather that makes this such fine grouse country, and up to a pair of distinctive double cairns atop the hill. Overnight downpours had soaked the ground but despite this the going was still good. Mind you, the legs got a real soaking from spray and I got chilly cheeks on some of the longer descents! Cresting the Height of Greets brought the twin rewards of a tremendous 360-degree vista and a third of the day's height gain already behind us. We took a break, admired the one and felt good about the other.

From here we had grouse shooting to thank for the improved track and, with rows of newly built stone butts in evidence, you were left in no doubt as to how much money was to be made from the cultivation of heather and feather. Back to biking. Enough rough stuff was left in the track to spice up the descent to Dent's Houses, with a fair few back-wheel skips and opportunities to loft front wheels a plenty. Another helpful landmark, in the form of a large shed, makes navigation really simple.

Apedale Road – a broad track – makes for an easy climb up Apedale Valley. We managed to top-cog, humming along two abreast until a short steep climb onto the moors strung us out. For the first time we met gloop. Typical peat moor stuff. A timid approach to one of those wet, black holes nearly put me over the bars but, apart from that, we reached and passed the cairn at Apedale Head with relative ease. The next half mile or so was up-beat, off-road entertainment – a mix of firm gravel track separated by black, gloop snares – before the trail started its dip down to the road near Hunt House Farm. Not too gnarly but rutted – just the right amount of rough stuff for some fun-time downhilling.

Take B6270 (E) to Low Fremington For 0.6m; on RH bend SO on lane 20yds. Turn L up lane to High Fremington for 100yds; L then R uphill to track 0.75m. N 1.5m over Fremington Edge to Hurst Farm. Turn L on bridlepath track 0.9m, then L (W) on single track to fence. R (NW) 0.3m to gate on inside of corner. Through gate, follow single track (WNW) to tips, swing L then R 1m on obvious single track to gate. Through gate to track 300yds to Storthwaite Hall Farm, R on track 1m to Langthwaite.

L over bridge, L (S) 0.75m on road to Raw. Bridlepath waymarked on R, head 1.5m (SW) then track swings (NW then W) round spur to Fore Gill gate. L through ford, up 0.4m to bridlepath track. Turn R (WNW) 1.6m uphill to

sheepfold. Keep L (NW) over Great Pinseat tips, follow cairns 0.25m; swing W 0.7m down to gate, through gate, L (S) through ford then down track 0.6m to Level House bridge.

R 1.2m across bridge, through tips on bridlepath track to fork; L (WSW) on single track, zigzag down through tips then S 0.5m onto grass by fence. Through fence

on single track (S) down Gunnerside Gill 0.6m to fields. Along grass track to buildings then track 1.25m to Potting fork.

SO 0.5m by wall, past Barf End Gate where bridlepath fades; keep by wall 0.5m to bridlepath junction; R (SE) 0.4m into field to track near wall. Turn L 1m (E) to lane to Feetham; L (E) on B6270 to Reeth for 3.5m.

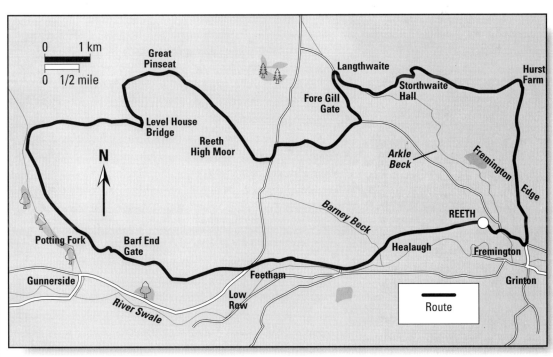

Down on tarmac to the High Lane bridleway gate, we crossed a field and dropped down a walled track to Low Houses in Swaledale. It was pretty rock-ridden in parts and festooned with flora. Surprisingly radical for a 'green lane'! The tarmac lane out of Low Houses felt like velvet after that lot but before long we returned to track on Dubbing Garth Lane. A lane of many guises – road, river-bed, swamp and savannah – Dubbing Garth delivered us onto the main road to Muker a might mucky. As we drew near to the village, the great dome of Kisdon hove into view; the track, snaking up its flank, looked near vertical. Not an encouraging prospect so a fuel stop in the pub was voted a good idea!

Refuelled and eager to take up the challenge of Kisdon we found our way through Muker's network of lanes to the way-marked track for Keld. The sun burst through the clouds and, just as we started honking, August arrived. Surplus heat again! Part dirt, part metal the track zigzagged up and up and this was the easy part! A welcome gate gave an excuse to dismount, then it was on and up again. Past Kisdon Farm we hit a precipitous grass/grit/rock ascent. Watched by a group of bovine spectators we toiled on. I was feathering in fine style on turf but the grit had me dabbing; Pete pedalled up all the way.

Close to the summit, on a sharp left turn, we took five and took in the view. Swaledale lay spread out below; 800 ft below! A 1:6 climb gets you up quick but knackered. Over the top it all got suddenly very Pennine-like – bleak high moor stretching round the horizon. The trail dipped gently and our speed over the cropped turf clocked up. Top-cog cranking, we really motored. Perfectly mannered pedestrians opened a gate when we got some serious gradient and we bounced down to Thorns Ford.

A short road ride to Keld then, just by the chapel, it was back to track concentration. Just as the Pennine Way got tucked in under the tyres, the path took a steep dive down to the river, slipped in some slick rock, a step and then some rough stuff. Brilliant! Lucky the gate was open!

Once across the Swale we climbed past the falls, departed the Pennine Way and hung a right for Crackpot and Ramps Holme in company with *Wheelwright's Coast-to-Coast* route. The sun had gone but we barely noticed as this bit of track is a fantastic run, especially down from Crackpot to Swinner Gill. First we hit a gnarly climb that tested line picking and power control to the limits, then came a tasty descent. There's just enough rut and rubble to make hammering a touch risky and, if someone opens the gate at Swinner Gill, a high-speed splash to kill the mph. Plus, the track runs down the side of a gorge so it's big air out right!

We elected to add in a final climb up Rowleth Heights – the sun

Kisdon's descent keeps this gnarly section hidden 'til the very end. Round the corner and it's cobbles everywhere

DIRECTIONS → → → → →   SWALEDALE SAUNTER

Take B6270 (E) over Grinton Bridge for 1m; SO 0.5m on lane to fork. R 1.1m to waymarked bridlepath on How Hill; 0.75m (SW) on faint then obvious singletrack to twin cairns, Greets Hill; through gate and (S) 1m onto track to Dent's Houses.

R (W) 2.2m on Apedale Head track to large cairn, 120yds after turn SW; 1.5m (WNW) to fence, swing R then L through tips, boggy single track, heading W then NW 300yds onto track to lane. Turn R 1m over grid, to gate at High Lane.

L 0.5m through gate, across field, through RH gate 0.5m onto Low Houses track. L 0.6m on lane to Haverdale; R 1.75m at 'dead-end' sign to follow Dubbing Garth Lane. SO B6270 2.5m to Muker.

R into Muker, L then R 200yds to waymarked bridlepath track. Through ford gate, track zigzags 0.5m to fork. SO (WNW) 0.5m up walled track, then keep wall on L, then walled track to gate, keep wall on R to corner. Turn L (W) 0.4m on grass single track through gates to sheepfold. More obvious grass track (NNW to N) 1m through gates, cross ford to B6270; R 0.4m to Keld.

R 300yds into Keld, R beyond chapel onto bridlepath. Single track 250yds to junction, then L 250yds to bridge, cross, L up single track to track above falls. Turn R (ESE) 2.5m on bridlepath track, keep R at Crackpot fork, to lane at Ramps Holme Farm. SO 1.5m to Ivelet, L 1.1m to Gunnerside.

SO (E) 275yds on B6270 to steel gate on L; through gate, 0.4m up drive, keep L of house, SO onto walled single track bridlepath. Keep SO (ENE) 250 yds, Heights House to R, single track keeps topside of wall; swing L (N) 200yds cross field up to gate. Through gate (SE then E) 0.5m to 1st wall corner on R; R 0.75m between walls to Smarber, keep L, through gate, follow track (E) to Low Row.

R (W) 0.25m on B6270; L 0.6m across bridge, L again to Low Houses. Turn L 1.5m on Low Lane track, lane (E) 0.75m onto moor. Bridlepath off L 50yds to 1st gate; R 1.8m on single track below Stubbins Farm, through gated fields to Swale Hall. On lane (E) 0.4m to Grinton to B6270 and, then L 50yds SO 1m to Reeth.

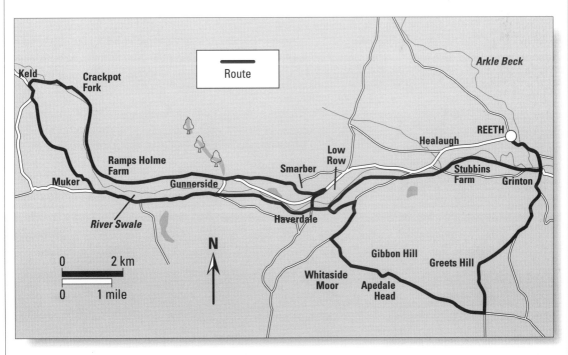

Taking to the tarmac on Malham Moor

Yorkshire folk call it God's country and when Nature lights the landscape, it's hard to disagree (far left)

Making mucky round Mastiles Gate – one of England's most renowned 'green roads' (left) was making a late come-back and we wanted a last look down on the dale. Up on the Heights we viewed 'God's country' by the light of a setting sun. As we were in the mood, we cut down through Smarber and on down to Low Row on bridleway to snatch an extra downhill. We then swung over Isle Bridge, hung a left and pedalled through meadowland to Low Houses and Low Lane track. Spinning along riverside trails made for an idyllic, summer evening's saunter in the saddle. A might too many gates on the bridleway section for my tired legs but we weren't in any hurry.

DIRECTIONS → → → → →

Start Malham Bridge (GR901629). At T-junction in front of the Buck Inn turn R (NNW) for 1m climb to gate with bridleway signpost. Then turn L (W) for 2.6m climb up obvious gated track (it zigzags a bit at first) past footpath signpost, over Kirkby Fell col then down to join Stockdale Farm drive.

Turn R (WSW) for 1.3m to C road T-junction then turn R (W) towards Settle for 110yds. Turn L (S) onto farm track bridleway for 1.3m past Blacks Plantation. Keep right at the next two T-junctions, to T-junction with C road.

Turn L (WSW) for 0.5m, skirting Settle village and keeping R at all T-junctions, to T-junction with unclassified county road track. Fork R (NE) for 0.75m up walled track then contour (N) in field, then between walls again and out alongside field boundary to gate.

Go through and immediately swing R (NE) for 0.5m (faint grass single track becomes obvious after 220yds) on gated single track, past woods to gate onto C road.

Go through and turn R (ESE) for 80yds to T-junction with unclassified county road. Keep SO (ESE then ENE) for 1.8m on obvious track past Victoria Caves, over col then swing R (E) alongside boundary wall (gravel gives way to grass) to stream crossing. Swing R (E) for 1.75m on obvious moorland track (boggy roller-coaster around Gorbeck but rideable) that gradually swings R (SE) finally climbing to two gates. Go through RH gate and continue (ESE) for 1m down gated track to C road.

Turn L (NNW), over cattle grid and immediately fork R (N) onto signposted bridleway track for 0.25m to turn R (ENE) through gate. Then SO (ENE) for 0.6m down obvious bridleway that swings L (N) to C road by Malham Tarn. Turn R (E) for 0.8m to go SO (E) at X-roads with unclassified county road tracks to gate. Then go SO (ESE), alongside wall, for 4.2m on Mastiles Lane unclassified county road over Holgates col, down steep descent to gate.

Go through and immediately turn R (SW) for 0.2m, between walls at first, to then swing L (S) for 0.5m to fork. (There are two or three vague tracks that meander about. Just keep climbing on the one along the bottom of the shallow valley west of Green Haw Hill.) Then swing R (SSW) for 0.4m, past marker-post, up to gate. Keep SO (S then SSW) for 0.5m, following marker-posts over hill, to gate onto C road.

Turn R (WNW then SW) for 1.5m, through gates onto bridleway drive, to Bordley Green Farm. Zigzag R/L (following bridleway signpost to continue W; effectively SO) through yard for 0.5m on obvious bridleway track that cuts across field corner to go through gate. Zigzag R/L across little valley for 0.7m to Lee Gate Farm gate.

Turn R for 140yds to T-junction and turn L for 2.2m, joining C road past Gordale Scar and Janet's Foss waterfall, to T-junction above Malham. Then go SO (W) for 0.25m down to the start.

Our Swaledale ride was nearly over but already we were planning a return trip!

CRAVEN CAPER

Distance: 25 miles. Climb total: 3600ft. Time: 4.5 hours (dry), 6 hours (wet).

Slippery when wet, it's a slick-rock limestone loop through a luscious lunar landscape.

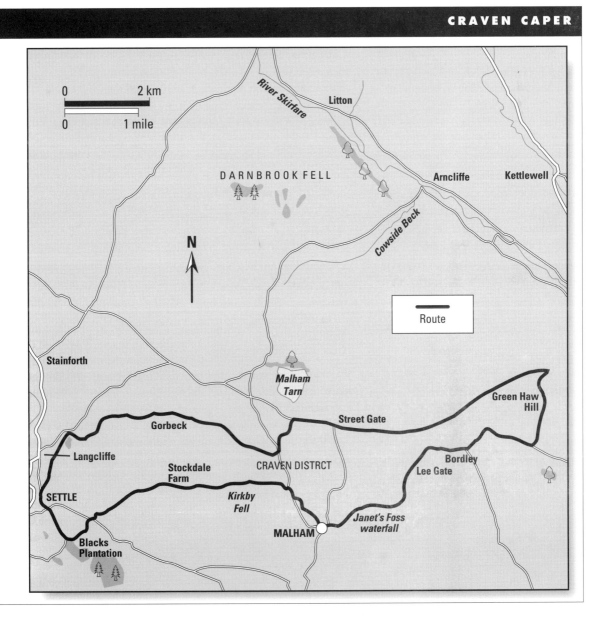

INFO: MALHAM MOORS

ACCESS

Malham's only directly accessible by road, though you can get a train to Skipton, Gargrave, Hellifield and Giggleswick or to Settle on the famous Settle–Carlisle line. Telephone 01228 44711 or 0113 244 8133 to book the bikes, then it's a ride of between 6 and 12 miles depending on where you alight.

Skipton, about 10 miles SE of Malham, sits on the crossing of the A59 NE/SW and A65 NW/SE trunk routes. From the SW exit the M6 at J31 and access Malham via Hellifield; from the NW exit the M6 at J36 and access Malham via Settle. From the NE go to Skipton via Harrogate and from the SE via Leeds then quit the A65 at Gargrave when Malham is signposted. There's a big car park (fee payable) at Malham for day-trippers.

MAPS

OS 1:50 000 Landranger Sheet 98 Wensleydale Wharfedale; OS 1:25 000 Outdoor Leisure 30 Yorkshire Dales – Northern Central and 10 Yorkshire Dales – South.

BIKE SHOPS

Nearest mega-bike shop is Stif (Tel: 0113 278 9606) just off the A660 Skipton road in Leeds.

We'd just conquered the calf-crunching 1000ft climb out of Malham, crested Kirkby Fell's col and now it was high time for some gravity suck, slipstream roar and fun-time, free-wheeling down Stockdale's ancient cart track. But we'd reckoned without winter's wet!

Broken bedrock limestone glistened in the rain. Suddenly we were slip-sliding down random rubble, the bikes skittish like broncos beset by buzzing flies, prancing and dancing down a slick rock slope. Too nervous to hit the anchors hard, we made vain attempts to cut the speed with discreet dabs at the brakes, hung onto the bikes and let them roll over the ice-like cobbles. Front wheels bumped and bucked, hell-bent on a wipe-out, but for every heart-stopping slither there was a heaven-sent hook-up then grip. A gate gave us some welcome respite from the unexpected radical edge to the ride. Not the un-technical scenic cruise that I'd described to Jacquie and Chris Marley on the way up the M1! And they nearly brought their tandem!

Slippery when wet – that's the Dales. So if you don't like putting your heart where your mouth is, tasting dirt from time to time and slipping along a trail with a technical edge, then wait for summer. Slick-rock limestone's got a lot of grip – in the dry. Meanwhile we tasted the delights of tarmac traction on the hum down Stockdale Farm's drive, before plunging into more cobbled cart track – this time with a coating of slime. Chris hit the first bend far too fast, did a speedway-style slide, foot dabbing danger-ously close to the wall, then he let out a whoop of delight as he carved a line through the curve and came out pumping cranks, home free! Nervous at first we were beginning to enjoy the unpre-dictable element that winter's wet was adding to our outing.

But scenics are the essential and uplifting element of mountain biking around Malham. They opened out above Settle when a brief spell of sunshine split the clouds, flooding the valley with warm light to rekindle latent sparks of summer. Meanwhile the incessant sausage-sizzling hiss of tyres on sodden turf, the fight for traction and the high fells hidden in mists were constant reminders that the day would be short, the ride long. Our route out of Settle was on county unclassified road but 'road' was far too grand a term for this grass track – a mud-plugger's dream, that dipped and dived through bog and beck round the bleak moors of Gorbeck. Jacquie was quite shocked that such a rutted, rudimentary track could be called a road! Obviously when I'd said that much of the riding would be on unclassified roads, she'd imagined there'd be more tarmac than mud. Labels aside, this waterlogged byway demanded complete concentration and once you'd plugged for a line, total commitment. Either you'd come up trumps and sail through, or the front wheel stuck in a sump of slurry and you'd be pitched head-first into peat. Line picking was a lottery and lack of experience was no handicap! We all wiped out more than once. Jacquie won the coveted flight ceiling record, with an endo and rut-ramming routine that almost put her arm in a sling.

Mastiles Lane – a renowned green road for 4x4 *aficianados* – had been crudely cobbled some centuries ago but long stretches are now reduced to serried ranks of sodden ruts. Wall-to-wall wipe-out territory and first to fall foul of the 4x4 legacy was Jacquie. A downhill dash added speed but not enough momentum. She ploughed into a bleak, brown lake, her wheels kicking up a brave wake as they disappeared from view. A brief hover, legs akimbo, Jacquie desperate to keep out of the mire then the inevitable dab. Dab? A decent, life-saving dab would have been fine, but Jacquie just pogoed sideways, did the splits and, just when we thought she was in for a bath, got her balance and hauled herself clear. Amazingly, a woman had just jumped out of a LandRover, camcorder at the ready and caught the whole performance on tape – she'd been well framed! Mastiles was in murderous mood and Chris came a cropper when a submerged stone stopped him dead and sent him headlong over the bars. Moral of the tale is don't ride the outside ruts where rocks, dislodged from the walls, lurk in the murk.

We let the LandRover get a good head-start – diesel fumes kind of foul up the atmosphere of dramatic landscape and fresh air – watching it see-saw off into the scenery and contemplating the conundrum that powered vehicles on fragile farm tracks pose. By the time we'd climbed Holgates Hill it was nearly lamp-lighter time and before us the road fell away in an enticing series of steps and bends. Empty as far as the eye could see, it was time to kick the cranks, feel the wind whistle and let the trail fade out in vision blur. At least that was the idea until the chain unshipped and I had to make do with a 40mph freewheel. Next time I'd spin out hard off the top, tackle the initial ramp of rough stuff and let gravity do the work on the run-out down to the gate.

Light was fading fast, making route finding round Green Haw Hill a touch tricky, but a handy set of blue-topped marker posts confirmed our heading and we made Malham Moor Lane without mishap. It was a relief to know that we'd got the obscure single tracking out of the way before darkness finally overtook us. Mind you, we had a compass and I always carry lights in winter – day rides often have a bit of night-riding tacked onto the end. Inadvertently or not! The dale's limestone tracks stood out starkly in the dark so we dispensed with the lights and let our night vision develop. That's until we took up on the tarmac lane beyond Lee

INFO: MALHAM MOORS

ACCOMMODATION

Accommodation ranges from camping, YHA, B&Bs, hotels etc. right through to luxury holiday lets. Malham YHA (Tel: 01729 830321) are well used to cruddy mud-pluggers. Be sure to book – it's a busy place. The Yorkshire Dales National Park (Tel: 01756 752748) office will send you an accommodation list or you can contact Skipton TIO (Tel: 01756 792809).

NOTES

The YDNP authority is in the process of revising the rights of way network and the status of parts of these routes may change. It publishes an annual leaflet *Path Changes* which is available from info centres or by post if you send an sae. Telephone 01756 752748 for more information.

A cyclist sweeps down to a Swaledale, bathed in the light of a summer evening's sun

Gate Farm. Quizzically called Smearsbottom Lane, we nearly re-christened it Wallwipe Lane after a few close shaves on the serpentine sweep down into Gordale Scar. Reluctantly – riding without lights adds a magical element that's instantly dispelled with illumination – we switched on. Immediately the lane was bathed in artificial brilliance. A moving pool of light that held us within the confines of our own bright cocoon. Only the streetlights of Malham dispelled the odd sense of isolation and it was then that I realised that it had actually been with me most of the day. We'd hardly seen a soul.

DIRECTIONS → → → → →

Start Malham Bridge (GR901629). Head uphill (NE) past YHA, for 2m towards Malham Tarn then fork R (NNW) for 0.2m on track to gate. Turn R (ESE) through Street Gate, alongside wall, for 5m on Mastiles Lane unclassified county road over Holgates col. Down steep descent (watch out for gate at the bottom!), over Cool spur to T-junction with metalled quarry road. Keep R (NE) for 0.4m to T-junction with B6160 in Kilnsey.

Turn L (N) for 1m, past Kilnsey Crag and over Skirfare Bridge, to T-junction. Then turn L (NW) over cattle grid for 6.25m up Littondale, passing through Hawkswick (tea room here), by Arncliffe and through Litton to T-junction with unclassified county road track.

Turn L (SSW) for 3.2m, turning R (W) immediately after crossing River Skirfare on New Bridge, on track above Pen-y-Ghent Gill valley to T-junction with C road. Then turn L (S) for 1.2m to T-junction with unclassified county road/Pennine Way by Dale Head Farm.

Turn R (NW) for 0.6m to T-junction by Churn Milk Hole, then turn L (SW) for 2m along Long Lane down to obvious track T-junction. Turn L (ESE) for 1.5m on roller-coaster Moor Head Lane unclassified county road/bridleway to C road.

Turn L (NE) for 0.12m to T-junction then turn R (ESE) towards Malham for 3m, through deep valley by Sannet Hall and SO (ESE) at next T-junction, to T-junction on LH bend. Go SO (ESE) over cattle grid for 0.5m to X-roads.

Take hairpin turn R (W) for 0.1m on very faint bridleway across field to gate, then swing L (SW then WSW) for 0.5m on bridleway single track (don't wander off line on sheep trails), over stream, past marker-post and on up to bridleway gate. Go SO (W) for 0.3m, by broken wall at first then swing L (WSW) just before field corner to cross another broken wall, over Black Hill col to gate (path does a lazy R/L swing for final 220yds). Go SO (W then WSW) for 0.4m on bridleway single track to T-junction with unclassified county road grass track (about 110yds E of a gate), then turn L (ESE) for 0.9m climb up to two gates. Go through RH gate and continue (ESE) for 0.5m down track to turn R (SW) just before gate. Climb for 0.8m on obvious bridleway over Grizedales, through three gates then up to and alongside wall to T-junction with track by gate.

Turn L (E) for 1.25m descent (goes through a series of bends near the bottom) to gate on C road into Malham. Turn R (SSE) for 0.2m (keep your speed in check) to LH bend then go SO (S) through gate for 0.8m, on faint bridleway across field at first then on walled lane. Down to track T-junction in Malham then turn L (N then NE) for 0.12m to C road in Malham and turn R (S) to start.

FOUNTAINS FELL FLING

Distance: 32 miles. Climb total: 3300ft. Time: 5 hours (dry),
7 hours (wet).

Grand tour through gorgeous terrain that finishes with a 1000ft
downhill fling. Kilnsey Moor kicks in with a fast-track descent
that delivers you breathless into the head of exquisite Littondale.
Barn-dotted and a sublime setting in autumn sun, you quit its
homely pastures on a leg-busting climb-out, to be greeted by the
imposing outline of Pen-y-Ghent. Track, tarmac and single track
put you on top of Kirkby Fell. Then it's downhill all the way home
– almost!

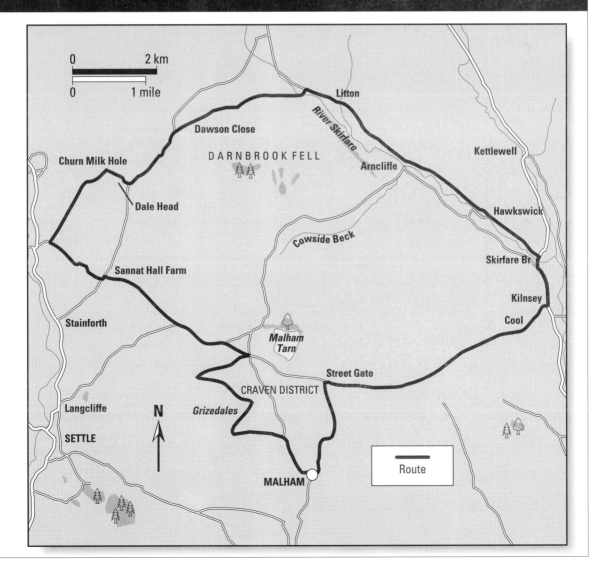

CHAPTER EIGHT

The Lakeland Roof of England

THE LAKE DISTRICT

Hammering down a gnarly descent smack amid spectacular scenery would be pure off-road paradise and, in England's green and pleasant land, if I had to pick a spot of paradise my map pin would impale a trail in the Lake District.

The Lakes are spectacular. Rugged crags and peaks rise up against dramatic skies, great fellsides sweep down into dales where the heights are mirrored in lakes and tarns of exquisite nature. Such sublime beauty is all too often missed by the likes of us – precipitous, rubble-strewn descents demand absolute concentration where a moment's distraction will spell disaster. Next to other wilderness areas, Lakeland's off-roading is in a class of its own – severe. Once ridden, the Cumbrian Mountains will draw you back into their fastness time and time again. Stretching skills, probing limits, testing nerve over terrain that's more akin to the Alps than the familiar high moorlands of these islands.

But to many folk, zigzagging down what amounts to a picturesque quarry side, playing cat-and-mouse with gravity and clinging to 25lbs of alloy is just a bad way to jump the hospital waiting list. Brain dead or what? So where in the Lakes can you find a good mix of routes? Something that'll keep the lunatic fringe happily vying for bed-space, while mere mortals like myself trail-blaze with just a touch of insanity as appropriate.

Derwent

On the northern fringe of the Lakes the broken, volcanic peaks of the Derwent Fells fetch up against the softer slates of Skiddaw (pronounced 'skidder') Forest. One is characterised by steep 'n' tricky single track, the other by forest trails and old mine roads. Between them is Derwent Water and the northern lakes' capital, Keswick. Keswick is a compact, bustling tourist town where you can step out of your B&B, hop onto the saddle and be dirt-tracking within minutes. On paper much of the riding looks pretty tame. Too short, too much road and too many tourists tastes, but plan your Lakeland rides carefully and they'll always prove spectacular to ride.

Ullswater

Not far east of Keswick is Ullswater. The eastern lakes provide a fantastic venue for off-roading which is why one of the toughest mountain bike events around – the International Polaris Challenge – has been held here. It's been billed the ultimate test of a mountain biker's self-assessment, strength and self-sufficiency. In it a thousand desperate bikers pit their wits and stress their skills in this awe-inspiring landscape of cloud-high horizons and rugged ravines. The two-day orienteering event offered participants an unparalleled opportunity to explore one of Europe's finest off-road regions. Craggy mountains cut a jagged skyline, cataracts gush crystal-clear water, deep green dales are bounded by swathes of burnished bracken and serpentine lakes – the sky in their depths –

Views over Borrowdale vie for attention on the radical drop down to Rosthwaite

reflect them all. Scenery aside – impossible in the Lakes I know – the off-roading is superb. Mind-warping switch back, single-track descents, roller-coaster ridge-rides with 1000ft of big air either side, gnarly technical track all sinuous and stepped plus road riding that'll burn your brake blocks off!

The Lake District National Park is doing its level best to take mountain biking on board – by hosting the Polaris Challenge for instance – and has done some pioneering work in accommodating our sport. We can help minimise the perceived impact of biking by riding the peaty paths north off High Street in times of low rainfall, or when they're frozen. In any event, don't be a wimp and perambulate round those peaty pools, pedal straight through. For details on the state of the trails, phone the local Park office (Tel: 01768 779633) before setting out.

BORROWDALE BASH

Distance: 17 miles. Time: 2.5 hours.

They ain't just knuckle-jarring gnarly – the descents on this loop are steep and twisty too. Ride every yard and you can count yourself as an elite expert.

This is a short but sweet couple of hours in the heart of the Cumbrian Mountains, with spectacular scenery if you dare to look up! The Watendlath to Rosthwaite leg gets rambler-ridden in

INFO: WEATHER

You'll be mountain biking in a wild and rugged region where wind, rain and height gain have serious implications for survival. High Street's crossed by England's third highest bridleway. Climbs – some 700ft – can take you into the clouds and maybe that forecast you missed might have forewarned you to forego the fell-tops and dally in the dales instead. Best by far, and at normal rates, is the Lake District National Park Weatherline (Tel: 01768 775757). For Cumbria's Weathercall phone 01891 500419 and Mountaincall is on 01891 500483.

A pastoral setting in the Derwent valley glimpsed from the Watendlath bridleway

season, so keep it for a summer eventide jaunt or a short winter sortie.

To be sure of minimum wait-time for walkers and maximum ride-time, we rode mid-week. Keith Pepper, our guide and a local rider keen on killer climbs, suggested a crack o' dawn start, so we set off just as amber sunlight cut shafts through the autumn mists that caressed Derwent Water's pristine surface. Talk about sylvan beauty but boy, was it nippy!

A lakeside road cruise followed by a twisty, tarmac climb up over Ashness Bridge sent a twinge through slumbering sinews. We were soon warmed up and keen to get stuck into some single track, but Keith insisted we take five at 'Surprise View' above Lodore. A surprise it was! A cliff-edge vantage point above one of Lakeland's classic scenes – fine sustenance for sagging, city spirits.

More narrow-lane snaking through autumnal fellsides brought us up to Watendlath – a farmstead now owned by the National Trust. You can tea-stop here but we gave it a miss, crossed the diminutive stone bridge and hooked up on the stone-strewn trail to Rosthwaite. Up ahead Keith picked his way through the scree with consummate ease – a skill natural to hard-core Cumbrian bikers. We southerners took it steady until the boulders had us beat and shanked the last 100 yards.

The flatter col gave a brief blast of easy cruising before a radical plummet into Borrowdale. My advice: take time out here to soak in the scenery before things get serious. In Keith's words, 'It's nay picnic lads!' – he wasn't kidding. Following his lead we splashed over a ford, coursed through an S-bend to slither down a section of ragged rock strata destined to suck you off left and into

INFO: KESWICK

ACCESS

Keswick is a prosperous tourist centre sited at the northern end of Derwent Water in northern Lakeland. It boasts all manner of facilities for the outdoor adventurer. The nearest BR mainline station is at Penrith; the 17 miles of A66 to Keswick aren't a pleasant ride but there are meandering minor road alternatives. By road, exit the M6 at J40 – Penrith – on the A66 west to Keswick.

MAPS

OS 1:50 000 Landranger 90 Penrith and Keswick or OS 1:25000 Outdoor Leisure 4 The English Lakes NW together with 1:25 000 Pathfinder 576 Caldbeck.

Languishing on Loadpot Hill after a day of off-piste pedalling on High Street

A 5m road warm-up kicks off at Keswick's Greta Bridge (GR263237). Go (SE) 200yds to pick up the B5289 Borrowdale road then 4.8m along Derwent Water's shores. Fork L (SSE) on C road for 2.75m, climbing past Ashness Bridge, Surprise View and on up to Watendlath Farm (NT café here).

Turn R (SW) across bridge, through gate and up over fell to Rosthwaite 1.5m away. (Steep, technically demanding descent with drop-offs, 'bike trap' gullies and roughly paved sections; lethal when wet!) On meeting tarmac keep R (W), over bridge and then L (S) on B5289 for 2m up first and steepest section of Honister Pass to 150yds past cattlegrid.

Pick up track paralleling road on R. Head (ENE), past sheepfold and downhill for 0.4m. Just past thorn tree on R fork L up singletrack (easy to miss and go onto gate instead) for 150yds to bridle-gate. Go through and follow obvious bridleway 1.8m to River Derwent. Technically very demanding sections will force most to dismount and the Castle Crag descent is gnarly so take care. Follow river downstream on track to Grange.

L (W) on lane for 0.8m. A boulder marks the start of the Cat Bells bridleway off L (NNW). After a steep, 400yd climb take the bridleway off R (N) for 1m along top edge of woodland, past seat then drop down to road, keep L on tarmac for 10yds then climb up steep single track L (N). Rejoin road after 1m. L (NW), over cattle grid and follow signs for Portinscale for 1.8m. In village fork R (NE) 0.2m, past hotel and cross River Derwent on foot-bridge. Continue 0.2m on to B5289 (there's a footpath alternative off to the R (E) and across fields to the town) and it's R (ENE) 0.5m back into Keswick.

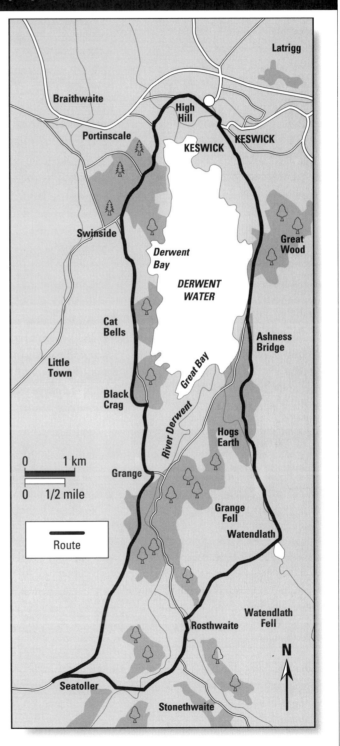

disaster. Keep well right until a step drops you into the loose stuff and you should be OK.

Down by a pine copse we paused, while a group of hard-pushed hikers struggled by. Then it was off again. The key to success was in hanging onto Keith's tail, shadowing every twist, turn, skip and jump. Absolute faith in his line choice was rewarded by a near faultless descent, high on adrenalin value and low on risk. It also gave the ramblers, goggled-eyed and open-mouthed, a tale to fill their postcards with.

Tarmac greeted us at Rosthwaite then it was road-rubber hum time to Seatoller and the bottom of Honister Pass. The road pitched to 1:3 and silence reigned as we resigned ourselves to a granny-ring hill climb. Over the cattle grid the gradient eased and I allowed myself a metaphorical 'pat on the back' – 18 months before Honister had me pit-stop part way up. Not this time! Back to track now for some well-deserved hammertime down Little Gatesgarth on a rough 'n' tough trail which kicked us in the tail a few times.

In a blur of fast-flying freedom we missed our left turn onto single track, met an extra gate and had to retrace our treadmarks. A quick map check confirmed that the overgrown path was bridle-way and we headed off across Scaleclose for Castle Crag on some brilliant single track. A touch technical with intermittent foot bridges and the odd, rugged unrideable section. Castle Crag sheltered some really rubbly stuff and, despite my leech-like adherence

INFO: KESWICK

ACCOMMODATION

Keswick is just one giant, Victorian medley of B&Bs with a scattering of multi-star hotels. Plus, of course, the YHA alternative. Despite the vast amount of bed-space pre-booking is essential in season. Keswick TIO (Tel: 01768 772645) provide a booking service for personal callers.

Skiddaw YHA (Tel: 01699 8325) is one of England's most remote buildings, offers basic, self-catering accommodation for hikers and bikers but is closed in winter. Mainstream YHAs are situated in Keswick (Tel: 01768 774129) and by Derwent Water (Tel: 01768 777246) where mealtimes are enhanced by classic lakeland vistas.

DIRECTIONS → → → → →

Start at Keswick's old station (GR272238) with over 4m easy off-roading along the Keswick Railway Footpath (KRF). Please give way to pedestrians. At 4.5m, just before 7th bridge, R through gate onto woodland path to road. L for 275yds then R, rejoining KRF to next road. R, 1m to Old Coach Road track with signpost 'Matterdale'.

Climb zigzag track, SO at X-roads, past old quarry and on to road 5m away. L to T-junction. L on A5091 for 2m. L onto lane for 2.5m via Wallthwaite (bends here!) to old A66 road. L up to new A66 then L (busy road) for 1.5m for R turn into Threlkeld. Go through village, past pub and church, for 0.3m to Blencathra Centre turn on R.

Steep, 1m tarmac climb to fork R just before Centre. 2m of track skirts Blease Fell, crosses valley bottom and meets Cumbria Way

bridleway (GR292280). L (S) for 2.5m on obvious path past Lonscale Crags (slick rocks, big drop! walk if your tyres are wet), through gate, over ford, through second gate and on into Latrigg car park. Follow signpost for Keswick bridleway through second gate on L. Obvious path (busy in season – give way to hikers) 1.5m down to road on edge of town. L and it's 600yds to start.

to Keith's rear rubber, a moment's relaxation and my bike was riderless. I was battered and definitely bruised but no bones broken. A lucky escape!

A gate marked the end of rough stuff and a saunter through sun-dappled wood delivered us into the centre of Grange. Tea shops, toilets and tourists galore. Keith didn't slow down, hung a left and motored off – we followed suit. We'd barely settled back into road-mode and it was off-road again. First up a bit of a killer climb on the flanks of Cat Bells and then across the back end of a copse on a narrow path, bounded by a crank-snatching stone wall. We came out into the open and were treated to Derwent Water, spread out in scenic splendour with Skiddaw beyond.

The Cat Bells bridleway was a ribbon of velvet by Borrowdale standards and, with long views ahead, we thrashed the downhills in fine style. Watch that dip back onto the road though, the return ramp up the Cat Bells bridleway is just a couple of crank turns away. All too soon the bridleway finished and we were back onto tarmac for the return leg to Keswick. A parched throat drew attention to a thirst that had gone unnoticed so far – definitely a great ride!

COACH ROAD AND RAIL CIRCUIT

Distance: 25 miles. Time: 3.5 hours.

A loop that's a medley of trail from mountain track to road and rail path. But this is the Cumbrian Mountains. What do you

INFO: KESWICK

BIKE SHOPS

Keswick Mountain Bike Centre (Tel: 017687 75202) where your hosts are themselves skilled trail-blazers. They'll mend your steed if you trash it, and their shop behind the pencil factory stocks everything you might need for a day in the mountains. Bike hire available also.

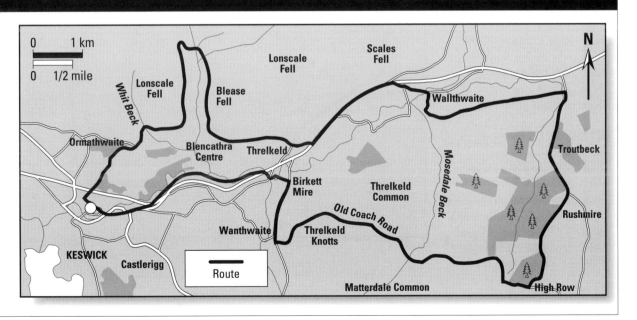

COACH AND RAIL CIRCUIT

expect? An easy ride? Not much – most of the road's an old coach road (a misnomer as no coach has ever got up this one!) that's a dose of traction-testing track and a craggy piece of single track, high enough to induce a tremble of vertigo.

SKIDDAW CLASSIC

Distance: 18 miles. Time: 2 hours.

A loop known locally as the 'Skiddaw Round' that kicks off with a lung-busting, 1000ft climb quickly followed by awesome technical single track that trips around Lonscale Crags. It'll test your trail skills to the limit. Beyond Skiddaw House a roller-coaster track delivers you onto a wind-whistling descent, known as the White Water Dash. Complete with switchbacks and techno-track, it's a drop to remember. By the time you cool off on

DIRECTIONS → → → → → SKIDDAW CLASSIC

Start Keswick hospital (GR264241) but try not to finish up here. Head N on A591 50yds then turn R (E) for 0.25m to T-junction with bridleway track and turn L (NE) for 1.5m climb to Latrigg car park. Zigzag R/L (effectively SO, (NE)) through gate onto single track for 0.25m then fork R (N) on obvious bridleway for 2.5m, down through ford, round Lonscale Crags (dangerously slippery when wet!) to bridleway T-junction below Burnt Horse. Continue SO (N) 0.5m on bridleway single track to gate then bridleway swings L (NW) 0.4m to pass in front of Skiddaw House YHA.

SO (NNW). Continue (NE) for 2.5m on obvious track to unclassified road (there's some fast, sometimes technical, descending but take on speed with caution – this is a popular walk). L (WNW) 0.9m to gate at T-junction with C road then L (SW) again for 1.8m to T-junction with A591. Turn L (S) for 4.75m to roundabout then go SO (S) into Keswick.

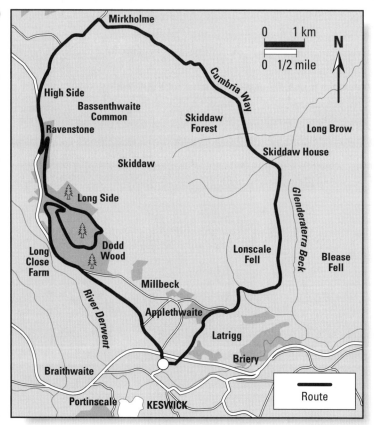

the tarmac return to Keswick you'll have had a great couple of hours in the saddle.

KIRKSTONE/HIGH STREET CAPER

Distance: 33 miles. Climb total: 4850ft. Time: 6.5 hours (dry), 8.5 hours (wet).

Prime bike territory where top-cogging, trail trials and topping out at 2700 ft will overspill the thrill quota.

To kick off with the Kirkstone Pass road climb is one way to sort the men from the boys. So Aaron, a long-legged teenager, led his elders – not betters – to the summit. A pub stop here seemed appropriate but in the event it was closed, so we continued on. Climb one and I was dead-legged already! Buffeted by a gusty force five we creamed down past Town Head, a cold slipstream singeing the ear lobes and Max Speed kissing 70 'clicks'. Now I know why roadies cruise the tarmac where it gets real tortuous!

The rocky track up past The Howe came as a rude awakening to the delights cf off-roading. At a backwoods meeting of the byways – we were on RUPP – we dipped left on an ancient highway, the legendary high road of the legions – High Street. No well-engineered paved Roman way exists now – it's all grit, gullies and gloop. Great stuff!

Wind assisted we'd cruised – mega-mires permitting – way up the Trout Beck Valley before the full import of the heights of the valley head and High Street hit us. Aloft, 700 ft of fellside loomed with a slippery, serpentine single track as the sole means of ascent. Or descent if you're daft enough!

We shouldered our frame sets, destined for an arduous carry. With the wind in ascendancy, slick grass and no grip, the carry to Thornthwaite was exasperating if interesting. And we all wore MTB boots with good aggressive grips so be warned! On top we took time to catch some breath and the views. Astounding, spectacular space cut by a rugged mountainscape that sweeps majestically south, down through dales to the sea. Shafts of light sliced the moist atmosphere where Helvellyn's height made ragged rents in a wind-torn cloud base. Nature put on a prime-time scenic display of splendid proportions. There's said to be a Laker in every Englishman and I believe it!

Aaron said it's downhill from here on. Not quite true but nearly so. The ravine carved out above Haweswater creates an awesome, yawning gap. Along its lip trips a tight piece of single track where an unexpected stack would treat you to a flight with your last rites as the ultimate endo. Only one way to go – fast. Keep the visuals firmly ground-bound and let the wheels take the air. Across the

The classic Lakeland scene known as Surprise View is a sight worth savouring on the Borrowdale Bash

Have bike, will carry. By far the quickest way up High Street is from Hartsop in Patterdale

Start Cow Bridge car park (GR402133) off the A592 by Brothers Water. For shorter 24m loop follow Caudale Moor Route to Straights of Riggindale. For the full blast go R (SSE) 7.5m on A592 via Kirkstone Pass to bridleway track off L (SSE), 110yds after Church (Trout Beck) Bridge. Climb past The Howe 0.5m to X-roads then L (N) down past Limefitt Park to ford and gate 2.5m away. Continue (N) on track (swing R through ford at 0.6m then keep SO at 1m) for 1.1m to gate.

Continue (NNE) alongside wall then climb 1m up fellside to cross spinal N–S Beacon–Ill Bell path. Safest route N is via Thornthwaite Beacon on your left, but bridleway actually goes SO over spur (NE then NNE) – with Gavel Crag scarp edge on your R at first – for 0.5m to wall. SO (NNE) on scarp edge W of High Street for 1.3m to go through another wall on Straights of Riggindale.

Continue (N) 50yds, fork R (NNE) then keep L (NE) onto less obvious single-track over Rampsgill Head and on (NNE) 0.9m over High Raise and down to Raven Howe to go through fence at corner. Keep fence on R for 0.4m then on L for 0.6m before veering R (NNE) 0.2m down off Red Crag through gap in wall. Keep L (N) for 150yds then swing R (NNE) on obvious single track for 1.3m to ruined chimney corner on Loadpot Hill.

L (NW then NNE) round W side of Loadpot Hill for 3.5m (ignore trail off L at 1.5m) to T-junction 150yds (W) of The Cockpit stone circle. L (W then WSW then SW) 3.25m (at 2.9m keep to upper grass track) via Mellguards (please walk past buildings), over ford/bridge to road. Cross road (WSW), climb round spur 0.6m to Martindale Chapel (swing round R at 0.5m).

On road L (SW) 100yds, fork R (SW) - watch steep bends here – over stream and R (NNW) at T-junction 0.6m from chapel. Fork L (W) onto bridleway after 0.5m. Sandwick–Patterdale bridleway is a popular ramble along twisty, technical single track – remember the Off-Road Code and give way to hikers. Follow Ullswater shoreline 3.75m (ignore path off L at 2m) to T-junction beyond Side Farm (please walk through this farmyard). Swing round R (W) on lane 0.3m to A592. L (S) 1.7m to start.

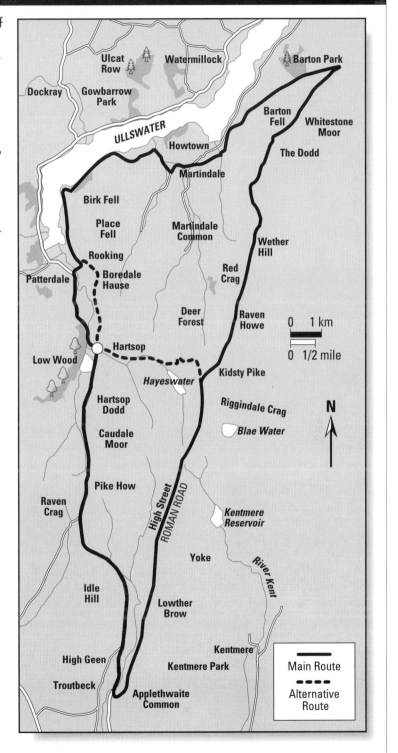

Derwent Water at dawn, seen from the Cat Bells bridleway on the Borrowdale Bash

Straights of Riggindale – Tolkien's got to have been here before – and up onto Raisdale.

The wind, winding up for a full-blown storm, had us all canted at a crazy angle and barely able to keep it all on the ground. Gravity sucks but not hard enough sometimes! Worries over one of us being blown over the drop-off alongside High Raise proved ill-founded – increased speed added stability. When we quit the rubble-ridden higher ridges for the peaty paths to Loadpot Hill, speed was the name of the game. Alone in a vast landscape – high winds had kept folk off the fells – we played tag on the 3-mile descent to The Cockpit. Endos aside – lower down there's one or two gloopy wheel-grabbers about – it's an exhilarating run!

From here to Patterdale, Ullswater underpins the views with a majestic sweep right into the heart of the Helvellyn range. The trail packed in some superlative single track, that must rate as one of the finest lakeside rides in the country. Shafts of stormy evening sun transformed our watery trail into shimmering, silver twin-track heading right for the dark mountain masses. We're talking spiritual experience here; Nature with a capital 'N'! Who said mountain bikers are nothing but yobbish speed freaks, careless of the country and ignorant of the wider view? Get a bike. Get moved!

Beyond Sandwick, with the sun already setting, we were treated to a tasty piece of technical single track that had a weary Aaron yelping with delight at each obstacle conquered. Entirely rideable

INFO: ULLSWATER

ACCESS

Patterdale is the pivotal point on these two routes. Road access is along the A592. From the south use J36 and the A6 off the M6 and take the A592 north from Windermere; from the north exit the M6 at J40 – Penrith – on the A66 west to pick up the A592.

Penrith BR station (Tel: 01228 44711) is just 5 miles from Ullswater's northern shore.

MAPS

OS 1:50 000 90 Penrith Keswick; 1 inch: 1 mile Lake District Touring Map 3 or OS 1:25 000 Outdoor Leisure 5 The English Lakes NE and 7 The English Lakes SE.

BIKE SHOPS

Patterdale is equidistant from Keswick, Penrith and Ambleside – each has excellent bike shops. In Keswick, the Keswick Mountain Bike Centre (Tel: 01768 775202) is tucked in behind the pencil factory in Dalestone Court. Ambleside boasts two serious off-road retailers: Bike Treks (Tel: 01539 431245) at 2 Millans Park and Gyhllside Cycles (Tel: 01539 433592) situated down in The Slack. In Penrith, Arragons' Cycle Centre (Tel: 01768 890344) is the place to head for and they're at 2 Brunswick Road.

Recently repaired by a local MTB work-team, this old miners' bridge is an essential link in the Coach Road circuit

yet challenging, the trail dipped and dived amongst the crags and crevasses. Below the lake, it's wind-lashed waters crashing on the shore, glittered where the scudding clouds let slip a pencil of light or two. Suffice to say we were tired, just about beat but definitely sad, when we made the final walk through Side Farm's yard and into Patterdale.

INFO: ULLSWATER

ACCOMMODATION
Accommodation ranges from camping right through to classy hotels. Dirt tracks start right from the doorstep. Details from Ullswater TIO (Tel: 01768 482414). The YHA is right in the thick of it at Goldrill House, Patterdale (Tel: 01768 82394).

CAUDALE MOOR CIRCUIT
Distance: 21 miles. Climb total: 4350ft. Time: 5 hours (dry), 6 hours (wet).

A couple of classic Lakeland passes – off-and on-road – sandwich the summit of England's third highest bridleway.

An eagle's eye view over Buttermere. The author and a trail-mate take ten on The Lakeland Loop long-distance ride

DIRECTIONS → → → → → CAUDALE MOOR CIRCUIT

Start Cow Bridge car park (GR402133) off the A592 by Brothers Water or Hartsop car park (GR410130). From Hartsop car park head ESE 0.4m to fork R (E) over bridge and climb for 0.7m. Fork L (E) across ford (fellside is criss-crossed by paths – your objective is to circle L round N side of obvious knoll, The Knott, 1000yds E). Carry/push (E) 650yds up across fell then L (N) 330yds to join major Angletarn–High Street single track. R (push/carry SE to E then S on rideable path) 0.8m finally down through gap in wall on Straights of Riggindale.

Continue (S) on scarp edge (W) of High Street for 1.3m to another wall. Safest route (S) is via Thornthwaite Beacon on your right but faint bridleway actually goes SO (S then SSW), with scarp edge on your L for 0.5m to cross spinal N–S Beacon–Ill Bell path. Continue (SSW then S) off spur now on obvious single track (steep 'n' tricky so take care) 1.1m through gate.

SO (S) 1.1m to fork L (SSE) through gate, over stream and on (S) for 2.2m to Limefitt fork. Keep L (S) 0.3m up to X-roads. (For excellent and optional Garburn ascent/descent detour turn L (NE) 1.8m to gate at Garburn Pass. Vista stop. Return 1.8m to X-roads.) Otherwise turn R (SW) down through R bend by The Howe 0.5m to A592. R (NNE) 7.5m over Kirkstone Pass – watch bends on descent – to start.

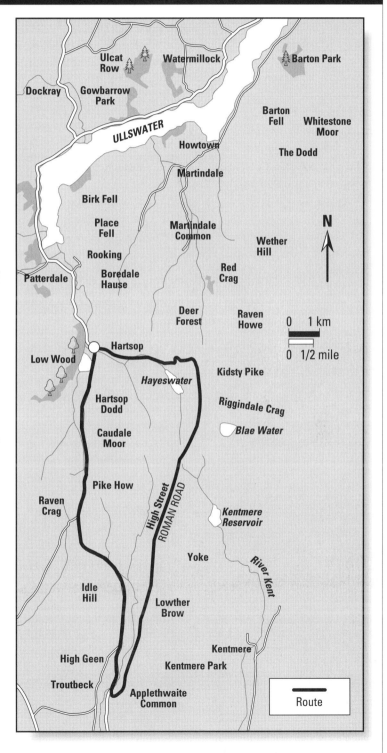

CHAPTER NINE

Cambrian Hill Country

WALES

The heart of Wales, where the Wye Valley cuts a deep rut in the Cambrian Mountains to create a rough and tumble terrain. A terrain that's a treat to ride. Seriously strenuous climbs put you on top of whale-back hills where you can stay all day, hammering hard pack, grass track and peat paths to your heart's content and all the while accompanied by expansive views.

On clear days, away on the southern horizons, the dark outlines of the Black Mountains and Brecon Beacons beckon hard-core bikers, but there's always an impelling, emerald-green valleyscape below and some fine track beneath your tyres. The riding's not technical but it can be tough. Especially when this land of the dragon is awash from winter's constant drenchers and there's a 1200ft climb stretching up and away from your front wheel!

Our rides are based in a duo of delightful towns. Llanwrtyd Wells (pronounced 'hchlanootid'), population 600 and the 'smallest town in Britain', was once a bustling spa town but accepts its retirement from fame gracefully – a bit like an ageing 18th-century dowager. Builth Wells (pronounced 'bilt'), an attractive market town, sits on the confluence of the Irfon and Wye rivers at the site of an important river crossing. Its position is the key to its continued success, and it remains a thriving community and town centre.

DIRECTIONS → → → → →

Start/finish in centre of Llanwrtyd Wells (GR879467). On A483 0.6m (ENE) to Cambrian Woollen Mill. L (N) through car park onto bridleway (signed footpath) between mill and house. 100yds and bridleway turns L (NNW). SO, 300yds to forest edge. SO (NNW) right through forest and on bridleway for 1m to join track. 350yds (NE) to Pistyllgwyn Farm and road. Road to Bwlchmawr, the next farm.

L (NW) through gate on bridleway track, keep R (NNW) at fork, through ford and on down to cottage 0.5m away. R (NE) alongside boundary, down to ford. R (E) 0.7m to spur summit. SO (NE) 220yds. Swing L (WNW) 400yds to ford Nant yr Annell. R (ENE) 0.25m up to spur summit.

L (WNW) 1m on bridleway track, keep N of hill summit, to gate by

Irfon Forest. SO (W) alongside forest, then between trees 1m to bridle-gate. Through gate, jig R then L (WNW) on single-track 250yds to fire-road. SO (NW) 75yds to gate on L. On moor parallel forest edge (NW) 220yds, swing L (WNW) 280yds to fence corner on Cefn Waun-Lwyd spur summit. SO (W) by fence 400yds, through gate (broken). SO (WNW then W) on bridleway single track 0.9m, crossing track, to Abergwesyn.

R (ENE) 0.8m on road. L (NW) on bridleway track 0.75m, passing Glangwesyn Farm, to gate. Swing R (NNE) on single track then track 1m to gate 30yds from forest at Cefn Garw. Through gate, R (SE), to T-junction 20yds inside forest. (Wet weather route is SO (SE), keeping to high ground and keeping SO when track swings L after 200yds, 1.4m to T-junction in

clearing. L (N) track zigzags then heads NNW downhill 220yds to fork above ruinous Fedw cottage. Hairpin R (SSE).) Turn L (N) on bridleway single track to fire-road. SO (NNE) 175yds on road. Swing R (NNE) on bridleway fire-break 0.3m to ford Afon Cammarch. R (ESE) 150yds to fence then by fence 0.3m to Pen Cae Farm. Through farm (S) 0.4m, crossing ford, to fork. Keep L alongside river 0.6m, up past Fedw ruin to fork. L (SSE) 2.5m, between river and quarry, passing house then Dolberthog Farm to join road beyond Llyn Owen Farm.

L (ESE) 275yds. R (SE) at fork above chapel 0.75m to A483 at Beaulah. R (WSW) 1.4m to fork. R (W) on lane to Bwlchmawr Farm then R (NW) through gate on bridleway track. Keep L (NW) and up hill at fork, for 1m to Irfon Forest East.

MAN V HORSE V BIKE VERSUS YOU

Distance: 29 miles. Climb total: 4200ft. Time: 4 hours (dry), 6 hours (wet).

If you're a fat-tyre fanatic and fit then why not take on the rough and tough Man v Horse v Bike race route? With 22 miles of Cambrian mountain track and over 3000ft of climb (some 1:3!) the course is, in a word, severe!

God favours the lunatic. Pale-blue sky spanned the 'roof of Wales' and under its eaves, golden sun flooded the sky where recent rains had flooded the valleys below. Rarer than the sight of a red kite in Kent, the warm light lifted spirits and spurred us into action. Overdressed, under-fit and with Red Kite's laconic guide, John Lloyd, along to keep the pressure on – we'd made a late start – we headed for the hills with 30 miles to go and just half a winter's day to ride it in.

Sunlit spray arcs out of a Cambrian ford on Man v Horse v Bike route

MAN V HORSE V BIKE

SO (WSW) 50yds. R (NW) on obvious fire-road 0.7m to fork. Keep R (SW) for 1m to barrier. SO (NNE) 400yds to junction. L (NW) 250yds down through dip to T-junction. L (W) 150yds to T-junction. L (SE) on main track 1.5 m, ignoring tracks off L, into valley and up far side to T-junction just past Cefn Crug summit.

Keep R (WSW) 2m on main track, ignoring side tracks, down to cross Irfon Bridge at picnic site (watch your speed!). L (S) on county classified road 0.4m to signed bridleway. L (E), ford Irfon River and pick up bridleway track 50yds downstream. 2m (SSW), keeping L at Altwineu Farm, to road just below Pont Newydd. L (SSE) 1m to start.

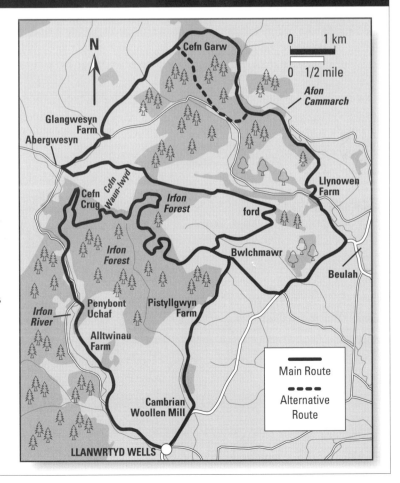

A brief taste of tarmac favoured us with one of the few bits of decent traction for the day before we dipped in behind the Cambrian Woollen Mill and hit the hills. With a splash! Surely this was a stream, not a path? Whatever, the watercourse snaked its way up into a dark, damp hole that was Y Foel forest. No sunlight penetrated the serried ranks of tall pines. The temperature dropped like a felled tree and I was minded of hobgoblins, hobbits and Tolkien. Creepy!

Out of the forest – me last and honking hard – to our first descent. Descent? Talk about freewheeling and you'll talk about track stands! Bog! And if that wasn't enough, the turf track climb past the ruins of Bwlchtuathrer turned into a granny-cog slog, through a quagmire reminiscent of school cabbage. Yuk! But hey! The sun's aloft and the view down the valley was exquisite. We took ten, savoured the scent of mountain air and watched while the warm rays wafted a couple of buzzards up on a thermal. Sheep dogs at Pistyllgwyn Farm favoured us with a baleful, pale-eyed glare; John disappeared pronto and we took off after him. At Bwlchmawr Farm we returned to track and climbed up the Einon Valley.

Sinuous single track snaked down to the stream with a tickle of technical to keep us on our toes. The switchback on this ford must be a nightmarish mêlée of speeding bikes, horses and runners on Man v Horse v Bike race day! Out of race-day reveries and back to the rolling resistance of water-logged pasture for the climb-out. Cefn Cynlliath's gritty track came as a welcome break and we were up on the pedals for our first off-road spin, over the spur and

INFO: LLANWRTYD

ACCESS

Llanwrtyd Wells is on BR's Swansea–Shrewsbury line, served by rolling stock with severely restricted bike-carrying capacity. Nothing runs on Sundays in winter and bikes have to be booked. BR at Cardiff (Tel: 01222 228000) have the details.

The M5/M6 spinal route is about 100 miles east with the best westbound links on the A40 via Gloucester from the south-west, the M50\A40 from the Midlands and the A483 via Shrewsbury (M54/A5) and Welshpool (A458) from the north. From South Wales use the A483 or A470.

MAPS

OS 1:25 000 Pathfinders 991 Beaulah Abergwesyn, 1013 Cilycwm Pumsaint and 1014 Llanwrtyd Wells or OS 1:50 000 147 Elan Valley Builth Wells.

BIKE HIRE

From the Red Kite Mountain Bike Centre (Tel: 01591 3236) plus guided rides.

Descending the side of Abergwesyn valley, amid a Welsh winter landscape

on for a precipitous plunge into another deep valley. Black ice – the unseen enemy – had me slip-sliding sideways but, in the space of a missed heartbeat, the front tyre bit and danger was history. Phew!

Atop Cefn Gardys a vista of Welsh valleys, clad in oak and pine, textures enriched by the slanting rays of a winter sun, invited us to amble. So amble we did, on some roller-coasting track – with stunning views all the way – that led us on to a mile of mire and millenia grass with the gradient set against us. But up here, winter had the land in an icy grip – waterlogged then frozen, the grass was as brittle as Shredded Wheat and we made Banc Paderau summit in good time. A navigational error had us floundering about in a snow-covered fire-break and lost us a precious chunk of time. When we did make it onto Cefn Waun-Lwyd moor, the route's high point at nearly 1500ft, our anxious guide took the lead and high-tailed it for Abergwesyn. Until a pool of peat pulled down his front wheel. Classic endo! Our amusement was justly rewarded by an endo each, in quick succession.
On to Abergwesyn.

Tarmac traction was bliss after the interminable battle against gloop, grime and gradient, but it was a short life on easy street. A 300ft climb over the shoulder of Bryn Clun soon strung us out. John, with an eye on the lengthening shadows, suggested a short cut down to the road but I was keen to complete the route. On we went.

More fire-break romping in Cefn garw forest – we foolishly ignored the wet-weather route up on the spur – brought us down to the Afon Cammarch 'ford'. Deep, fleet and freezing, the crossing numbed the toes but we were buoyed up by John's announcement that, 'It's downhill all the way home boys!' Not strictly true and, given that we still had to negotiate riverside bogs, ice-covered pine poles, spanning streams in spate and run the gauntlet of not-so-friendly farm dogs, we still had a way to go before hitting the road at Llwyn Owen. But get there we did and in winter dusk, with blackbirds trilling from the hedgerows, we cruised back through Beaulah and took the A483 home. John reckoned this was one of the toughest rides he'd tackled. I agreed.

CWM HENOG HIKE

Distance: 24 miles. Climb total: 3000ft. Time: 3 hours.

If wet Welsh weather persists, then forsake the high fells east of the Irfon Valley and head for the firmer forest trails of Cwm Henog Plantation to the west. Here the fine sweeping fire-roads, big climbs, sizzling descents and a provident pub stop halfway, prove ideal for a mid-winter foray.

Ancient tracks abound in mid-Wales and, like this one above Cnyffiad, they seek the high ground

INFO: LLANWRTYD

ACCOMMODATION

We're spoilt for bespoke accommodation because the Red Kite Mountain Bike Centre at the Neuadd (pronounced 'niath') Arms Hotel is right in the centre of town. Mud, sweat and gear are all in a day's work for the helpful staff.

Don't want to rub shoulders with fellow mud-pluggers, talk bar-ends all night and have to hide that stiff-limbed hobble up the stairs? Then try Bryn Poeth Uchaf Farm YHA (Tel: 01550 5235) (GR797439) near Llanerchindda. It's remote, pretty basic and open from March to October. Other accommodation can be found via the local TIOs at Llandovery (Tel: 01550 20693), Builth Wells (Tel: 01982 553307) or Brecon if it's mid-week in winter (Tel: 01874 622485).

NOTES

Routes described are subject to the usual restrictions/permissions from the Forestry Commission, so please check locally at Llandovery (Tel: 01550 20394). There's also a vehicle speed limit of 16mph on these Forestry Commission tracks.

Ideal too for the four lads up from South Wales for a day's guided trail-shredding in the Cambrians with Red Kite's John Lloyd. So we tagged along, letting him sort out which track was what – one's much like another out there.

A short spin up the Abergwesyn road before we swapped tarmac for watery single track down by a mill – I got a feeling of déjà vu as memories of the Man v Horse v Bike route rippled by. A feeling reinforced by another ice-dip ford, then a push up a boggy trail riddled with random rubble. Up to the ankles in mud, it hadn't sunk in that we'd be sliding down this on our return.

Relief at reaching firm forest road was tempered by John's announcement that we now faced a 2mile climb. Way below, a red kite cruised between the trees and I chalked up my first sighting. Winter's often the best season for wildlife spotting. On and up. Past the 1000ft contour and beyond the snowline our track snaked through the trees.

With 'hill 1' dead and buried we took five, savoured the sight of cinder track, stretching away downhill and set off. But this dip was just a taster of the trail thrills to come. Out on the flank of Fwng – big valley space out right – the track dipped, we spun cranks and mountain air whistled through wheels spinning at warp speed. A series of slow bends was spiced up with a cambered chicane, John lost the lead and his over-keen clients screamed past our turn at Fwng-Uchaf Farm. After the re-call we renewed our acquaintance with ruts and rubble, before the leg-busting road climb by Llanerchindda.

The Royal Oak at Rhandirmwyn (pronounced 'randermoyne') provided a welcome pit-stop – bikers have to have a bevvy somewhere – before dropping down across the river and up the magnificent Tywi (Towy) valley. Water cascaded down the fellside in wild cataracts, fit to grace a calendar. And they have done.

High-flying bridleway above Builth Wells on the Cwm Owen circuit

DIRECTIONS → → → → →   CWM HENOG HIKE

Start/finish in centre of Llanwrtyd Wells (GR879467). On Abergwesyn road (NW) 1.5m over Pont Newydd, up, SW of chapel, to Dinas Mill.

Fork L (WSW) just past mill down single-track bridleway to Nant Henog ford. SO (W) then swing R 220yds up to track. L (SSW) on bridleway track for 1.5m fire-road climb to T-junction on Cwm Henog.

L (WSW) 0.5m to fork below Cnapau Hafodllewelyn. L (SW) on track for 3m, along NW side of Fwng spur, to Fwng-Uchaf Farm. Fork R (SSW) down to road. R (W then N) over bridge and 1.5m to RUPP track.

Fork R (W) and swing R 0.4m to road. R (N) 3m, via pub at Rhandirmwyn, to Gallt-y-bere fork. L (NE) 120yds, over bridge then hairpin R (ESE) 1m to cross 2nd bridge. 0.75m to Troedrhiw Ruddwen Farm.

R (NE) up track 1m to fork. Hairpin R, 1.2m across dam to T-junction. R (S) 330yds on road to fork. Hairpin L (ENE) 1m to fire-road off R (ENE). 2m, zigzag climb on main track (first swing is R) to T-junction at Croes Lwyd Fach.

R (SW) 1.4m to fork below Cnapau Hafodllewelyn ignoring side tracks and passing small quarry on L. Return on outbound route to start.

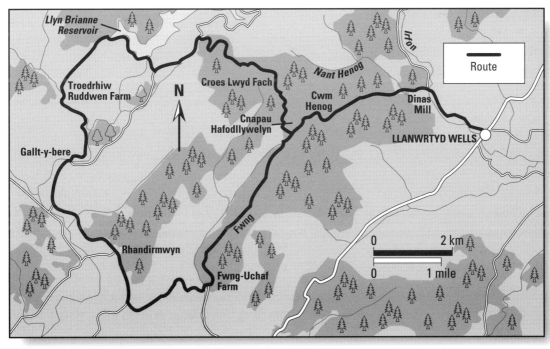

ACCESS

By road it's about 70 miles west of the M5 and Worcester, and 55 miles north of Cardiff. Allow plenty of time as the roads are pretty tortuous.

MAPS

OS 1:25 000 Pathfinder 1015 Aberedw and 992 Builth Wells.

ACCOMMODATION

In Builth there are plenty of places to stay. The TIOs at Builth (Tel: 01982 553307) or Brecon (Tel: 01874 622485) will be pleased to put you in touch with accommodation, which ranges from campsites, farmhouse B&Bs through to top-class hotels. There's no convenient YHA. And if you're worried about what to do if it rains then there's a plush sports centre and climbing wall.

Cambrian cart track climbs north from Troedrhiw Ruddwen Farm and it was a challenge to make the summit without a dab. We did. Just! Our legs found relief on the drop down to the Brianne Dam – spectacular water spouts are a sight to savour if it's not sleeting – but those spent limbs didn't realise what was in store. The forest at Mynydd Trawsnant concealed a 500ft fire-road climb back into the snow. Too shallow a slope to honk, it was a 'get down and grind' climb but the reward was a fitting finale to the ride. Once the wheels felt the finger of gravity pull, it was a quick freewheel to recover, then two miles of forest fire-road flashed by. Hill climbs were forgotten as trees whizzed by in a blur, and all too soon we were humming down the road, back to the Red Kite Centre and a fireside whisky.

LLANDEILO LOOP

Distance: 22 miles (33 miles from Builth via Aberedw). Climb total: 3500ft. Time: 3 hours (dry), 4.5 hours (wet)

The ride kick's off with a calf-singing climb up some steep, single track to the summit of Llandeilo Hill. Luckily it's a whale of a hill so once you're up, you're up – for most of the ride anyway. All you have to do is hammer or amble as the mood takes you and enjoy the majestic panorama over the deep green Edw Valley, nigh on 1000ft below. In summer it's idyllic. A broad sea of purple, scented heather and a heat haze to blur distant horizons.

CWM OWEN CIRCUIT

Distance: 24 miles. Climb total: 3,200ft. Time: 4 hours (dry), 6 hours (wet).

When you kick off with a 1200ft climb, you know you're into some serious cycling.

Cwm Owen (pronounced 'cumowan') is a loop that local riders view with respect. Especially in winter. I looked up at the dark clouds scudding across storm-lashed moorland. Forecast ferocious, outlook ugly. A good thing John Lloyd, our local guide, was along to keep us on track.

For the umpteenth time we were toiling up hill, into the wind, rain stinging our faces, frowning against the furore and once again I was tagging along as tail-end Charlie. Already we, or at least I, had cruelly tortured calf muscles on the tarmac climb to access the Wye Valley Walk (and come to think of it, why weren't we walking?) across Alltmawr. In the clamour I just caught the gist of John's words as they flew past 'You can see right down the Wye Valley from here ...'. Visibility about 400 yards and falling and my imagination was failing. Somehow I couldn't picture splendid scenery, just morbid moorland, windswept as in a Bronte epic. Silently I thanked myself for fitting a 24 granny for this trip. It looked like being the only gear I'd be grinding today! Boy, was this grass sodden and the landscape looked like the tide had gone out. Just!

Even in the face of such adversity there's an element of fun. Well, perhaps not fun exactly, more a sense of satisfaction that Nature's doing her best to beat you into the earth but you're holding your own in a war of attrition.

A dozen miles later and we were lost. A combination of local knowledge mismatched against the map, low cloud (like at ground level!) then failing to stop and plan a strategy to find ourselves again. Not easy when there's nothing but a blank wall of white beyond your bar-ends. A bit of dead reckoning plus pin-pointing our height with an Avocet Vertec (a nifty little wrist barometer). Then all we had to do was find a field boundary – which we did – then follow it to a farm access track – which we did – then leave the storm-tossed hilltops behind. Which we did. We surprised a farmer though – he thought we were mad to be out and perhaps he was right!

The first tarmac descent and we were flying down to Gwenddwr on a good dose of gravity suck. No head wind, no

The pristine surface of Pant y Llyn in the light of a frosty morn

rolling resistance! Mind you, Panaracer Spike tyres on slick wet tarmac aren't the ideal treads to shred the bends. A bit slip 'n' skippy! Funny how a brief bit of slipstream blast can put the world to rights and before long we were back on top, the wind now behind us and whipping along, tyres sizzling in the slurry like sausages in a pan. Once we had the lake of Pant y Llyn in our sights we knew that, bar a brief(ish) tarmac climb, it was a downhill blast all the way to Builth. Five miles of well-deserved fun time!

INFO: BUILTH WELLS

BIKE SHOPS

For the aspiring off-roader looking for a warm welcome in the valleys, Builth Wells Cycles (Tel: 01982 552923) in Smithfield Road is the place to head for. The staff are keen and accomplished mountain bikers and run guided tours in the Cambrians.

NOTES

Some of the riding is over grouse moor so access may be restricted at times in the shooting season.

Thankfully carries are few and far between. This one's on the Man v Horse v Bike route

Start Llandeilo Graban (GR094447) (parking severely restricted here) and head NE for 0.5m to T-junction with bridleway track.Then turn L (NNW) for 0.5m, past Blaenhow, alongside field boundary to track junction. Go SO (NNW) for 0.25m, following power lines, to X-roads on spur. Then turn R (NE) for 1.5m above the Edw Valley on single track, going SO (NE) at track X-roads just after Glanau Pool, to Twm Tobacco's grave (marked by a small wooden post).

Continue SO (NE) 200yds then hairpin turn L (W) for 0.2m to turn R (N) for 0.8m on steep descent, keeping L (NNW) as you approach Pentwyn, to the Aberedw/Rhulen C road in the Edw Valley. Turn R (E) for 2m to the 1st T-junction (phone here) then turn R (for Rhulen and Painscastle) for 200yds to next T-junction. Then turn L (E then ESE) for 0.5m to T-junction just past Rhulen Chapel.

Turn R (NE) for 1.3m, SO (ENE) at T-junction then past Pentre for steep climb up valley on BOAT passing Doctor's Pool to track X-roads by Pwll Brwynog puddle. Keep SO (E) on obvious BOAT track for 1.5m, finally to go through gate then down to tarmac, to T-junction. Fork L (NE) on gated BOAT for 0.6m across ford and up to T-junction with C road.

Turn R (S) for 2.25m, keeping R (S then SSW towards Painscastle) at Bryngwyn Green and R (SSW) at T-junction with B4594, to staggered X-roads in Rhos-goch. Turn R (W) up Perthycolly Valley for 1.1m to T-junction and turn L (W then WSW) for 1.1m, over cattle grid then up over spur, to X-roads with C road.

Turn R (NW) for 2.25, over col by Ireland's notorious knob (there's a tempting green lane short cut onto Rhulen Hill – please ignore it) and round Rhulen horseshoe, to X-roads on sharp R bend. Take hairpin turn L (SE) for 0.5m steep (there's a less steep alternative track that heads SW then S) to track T-junction above a ford. Turn R (SW) for 1m to another bridleway T-junction on col (puddle-ridden in winter) and there fork R (W) for 0.3m, finally down dip. Fork L (SSW) off track for 0.4m, crossing stream and col on your R, and down to track T-junction.

Here turn L (S) for 0.5m on bridleway down valley to C road. Turn R (WSW) for 2m, going SO (SW) at T-junction, to start.

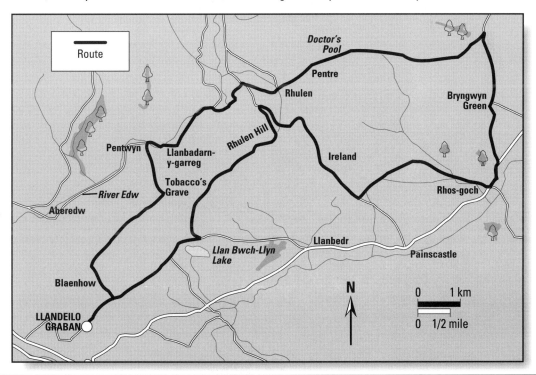

A scenic saunter above the Wye valley. Idyllic in the sun but in winter's wet, the Cwm Owen circuit is a killer (left)

**Sunset over the Wye valley, in
the heart of Powys (above)**

**Once you crest Banc y Celyn it's
downhill all the way to Builth.
Well nearly (top)**

The inclement weather meant we had it to ourselves. Out and out downhilling! A heady mix of greasy grass, rut, rubble and bed-rock, this trail had a demon lurking in every twist and turn. It was wet like a river. This super-saturated, slippery serpent was more like an eel to ride. Edge of the envelope, adrenalin-inducing stuff and it was inevitable that there'd be a wipe-out. My other riding companion Chris, hot-dogging John on the last, fast blast into Builth, carved into the final bend hell-bent on picking off the

D I R E C T I O N S → → → → →

Start Builth Wells Cycles (GR039509), turn L (N) 25yds to T-junction then turn L (W) to follow one-way system clockwise for 0.5m. Back W through high street, to take hairpin turn L (E) then immediately turn R (S) onto B4520 (heading for Llanddewi, Upper Chapel and Brecon). Continue (S) for 1.25m then fork L (SSE) for 1.4m, keep L (E) after bridge, to X-roads with bridleway/RUPP tracks. Then turn R (SW) for 0.2m up track to go through gate SO (SSE then WSW) for 0.2m, through another gate, to emerge onto moorland by waymarker and pool. (Bridleway track now roughly parallels field boundaries on your left on a meandering route for 2m to a road.)

Climb (S) for 0.3m to then swing R (W) for 250yds then turn L (S then SSE) for 0.5m (gets muddy along here). Turn L (SE) round field corner with pine copse adjacent. Continue (S) for 0.6m, through two fords, to waymarker then swing R (SSW) for 0.7m to fork. Keep L (SW) for 0.2m to bridleway X-roads with C road at Waun Hirwaun.

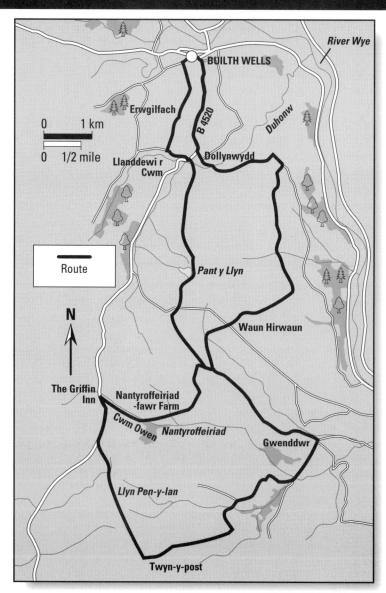

flying Welshman. (He'd already outclimbed John on the last hill but John pipped him into this final run-out.) Ahead lay twenty yards of algae-encrusted slate. A smooth, slick rockslide that glistened evilly in the gloom. Chris hit it hard. Both wheels whipped away, the bike spun and Chris flew. Unlucky! Ground contact came as a knee-jarring crack. Ouch! No bones broken but a week or so later it was still an elevated limb and ice-packs for him. Riding Welsh hills in winter ain't no pootle!

CWM OWEN CIRCUIT

SO (WSW) for 0.4m, immediately through 1st ford, to swing L (S then SSE) just after 3rd ford for 0.4m climb to yet another ford. 50yds after it turn R (SW then W) for 0.25m, passing by thorn tree then joining green bridleway track. Then turn L (S then SW) for 1m, contouring up shallow valley then over spur and keeping R (SW) at vague T-junction, with a steep descent down into valley above Nantyroffeiriad-fawr Farm.

Turn R (NW then WSW), climbing at first, for 1.1m across Nantyroffeiriad stream and up Cwm Owen track to B4520 (the Griffin Inn is just 200yds down the road). Turn L (SSE) for 0.5m climb to fork L (S) onto bridleway (obvious at first then vague twin track) for 1.6m, simultaneously passing below power lines (100yds W of where they turn from S to SW) and over stream. Climb low hill by Llyn Pen-y-lan (a seasonal pool) and on a SSE heading up to Twyn-y-post bridleway X-roads (a pine plantation is now 0.6m up ahead of you).

Turn L (E then ENE) for 1.4m, descending gradually at first on faint single track then more steeply down spur with small valley on your R, to bridleway T-junction at field boundary. Then turn L (NW then N) for 0.25m down beside fields to track T-junction then swing R (ENE) for 0.2m, up past farm to T-junction with C road. Turn R (ESE) for 1.7m, contouring at first before steep drop into valley and out again, to staggered X-roads in Gwenddwr.

Turn L (WNW) for 1m, keeping L past church then SO (W) at T-junction on R bend, to T-junction with bridleway track. Turn R (N then immediately NW) for 1.25m, keeping close to field boundary on your R, along top of spur and rejoining outward route, to familiar bridleway T-junction where you previously turned L (S). Keep SO (W) for 0.5m, over col, to track X-roads then make hairpin turn R (NE then keep N) for 0.8m, on roller-coaster trail. Finally up short climb to bridleway X-roads with C road.

Go SO (N) for 1.1m, to pass round E shore of Pant y Llyn Lake on single track then dip through ford, to obscure fork when grassy track begins descent. Swing gently R (N) for 0.25m to gate (if it's wet watch your speed and keep to shallow gully or you'll hit the tricky drop-off on the left side just before the gate). Continue (N) for 0.6m down gated track to farm (take extra care here), then SO (NNW) for 200yds to staggered X-roads.

Go SO to zigzag L/R (effectively SO) (WNW) for 1.6m, keeping R (NNE) at next T-junction, down to T-junction in Builth. (Take care – you may meet horses/hikers coming up, and there may be children playing at track terminus.) Turn R (ENE) for 0.2m to A483 then zigzag R/L (effectively SO) to follow one-way system for 0.5m ride clockwise back through town to Smithfield Road, then turn L (S) back to start.

CHAPTER TEN

Banks and Braes

SCOTLAND

Ardent Sassenach MTBers, minds filled with awesome images of Highland mountainscapes, hurtle through the Scots Borders with barely a glance at the towering fellsides that beset the old A74 Glasgow route. Further north, fat-tyre freaks from the mean streets of Glasgow head into the far-flung glens and braes for their kicks. It seems everyone's image of the ideal off-road venue in Scotland is way, way up north. But it needn't be.

INFO: GALLOWAY FOREST

ACCESS

Newton Stewart and Minnigaff make ideal bases but access is limited to road. Newton Stewart's on the A75 Stranraer road 70 miles from the A74/M6. From the north take the A702 off the A74 then the A712 from New Galloway.

MAPS

OS 1:50 000 Landrangers 77 Dalmellingon to New Galloway and 83 Newton Stewart Kirkcudbright; Special Edition OS 1:50 000 Landranger Galloway Forest Park (available from Polaris International Challenge (Tel:01246 240218) or Forest Enterprise Clatteringshaws and Glen Trool Visitor Centres).

ACCOMMODATION

Details from Dumfries TIO (Tel: 01387 53862), Minnigaff SYHA (Tel: 01671 402211) or you can camp at the Forestry Enterprise (Tel: 01671 402420) campsites at Talnotry or Glen Trool.

Right on England's doorstep and carefully misnamed the Lowlands, those lofty hills are anything but low. Trig points commonly dance above the 2000ft contour and fellsides sweep into the Solway to mirror the Cumbrian mountains on the far side. Homeland to two Scots passions, the battle and the ballad as espoused by natives Robert the Bruce and Robbie Burns, Galloway is a land of rich contrasts. Its Forest Park's sea of deep green pine is punctuated by the crags and crevasses where hundreds of miles of tracks are ours to roam. Riggs and Thinns rise abruptly out of a rolling sea of larch forest; dramatic, craggy and clad in winter colours of gold and cimmerian grey, these isolated islands are populated only by wild goat and raven.

But the Galloway Forest Park is no park in the urban sense. Massive – it virtually fills a 600 square mile OS 1:50 000 sheet – and full of contrasts, the Galloway's mix of remote ruggedness with rolling pine plantation has provided both Polaris and Karrimor with a testing venue for their internationally renowned challenges. Yet, in summer, families are drawn to the forests to enjoy a languid weekend of quiet strolling along shade-dappled paths.

Closer to Scotland's big city belt lies Crieff, an old market town clinging to the Knock. A hill that's a last Highland fling in the magnificent mountainscape which steps south from the grim fastnesses of the Grampians. North of the Knock the Highlands begin in earnest with a bevy of moody Munroes (you can actually see a dozen from the Choinneachain cairn, a high point on one of our loops), rugged ridges bedecked by dazzling white patches of summer snow, green glens and glittering lochs to mirror the mountains against an ever-changing skyscape. Crieff came to grief and got burnt to the ground in a Jacobite rising, was rebuilt in the 18th century, became an important cattle-trading market – hence the convergence of drove roads – then its spa gained prominence in the 19th century and Crieff's catered for the tourist ever since.

FLEET FORAY

Distance: 18 miles. Climb total: 1250ft. Time: 2 hours.

Dual purpose daytime/nightride glide through pine plantation with golden Galloway braes as a recurring backdrop.

It's February. It's bitter but dry and, with an eye on the Arctic weather front freezing southern England and romping northwards, we opted to explore 30-odd miles of Galloway Forest track on our first foray into the trees. Tightly stacked contours give the sage-green map of Clatteringshaws Forest an earthen hue; despite the craggy country, nearly all the tracks climb the hills contour by contour in gradients of gentle nature, so we felt duty bound to add

DIRECTIONS → → → → →

Start at the Clatteringshaws Forest Wildlife Centre (GR553766). On A712 go R (WSW) for 1.2m, over River Dee Bridge. Then L (SSE) into forest for 0.3m to fork R (S) onto Meikle Cullendoch track. Continue 6m, keeping L (SSE) at Grannoch Lodge T-junction and down by Big Water of Fleet River, to T-junction signed 'Loch Fleet'. Turn L (NNE) for 2.75m, passing Loch Fleet track on the L, to T-junction. Turn R (S) 0.8m down to T-junction then L (NNE) 1.2m, ignoring minor track off L, to next T-junction above Glengainoch Valley. Turn L (NW) for 2.1m to X-roads then go L (NW) for 4m to A712. Return R (NNE) 1.2m to start.

Cruising down the Knocknevis track in Galloway Forest

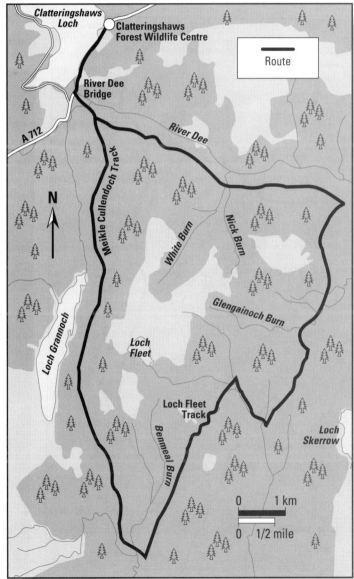

INFO: GALLOWAY FOREST

BIKE SHOPS
Ace Cycles (Tel: 01556 594542) in Castle Douglas.

NOTES
Forest Enterprise promotes waymarked off-road rides but it regularly hosts rallies, trail quests, army manoeuvres etc. plus there are often timber operations that close/divert routes so phone before you go to get the latest info. Its offices can be contacted on 01671 402420 and 01556 3626.

A Glentrool trail in saunter mood

in a few detours where track, terrain and gradient were at odds.

I'd been cooped up in a car for over six hours so I was off into the forest, filling the lungs with fresh mountain air, in fine fettle. It's tempting to wax lyrical but MTBing frees the spirit and early ride times have moments worth savouring. A quick regroup and we set off between the deep pine stands, cruising through ice-capped puddles with a satisfying 'crrunch' and keen to hit the first downhill.

A quick stop to savour a stunning view of Loch Grannoch, glimpsed between the trees then we let gravity tug the tyres on a long descent to the Big Water of Fleet. Sounds like Indian country – looks like it too. But who'd let gravity do all the work? Front wheels were soon vying for front place, rubber hummed, ice zip-cracked in water-filled ruts and it was a hum-time down to the chicanes in the valley bottom. Nature had us stop to take in a back-lit riverscape hemmed in by marching pines and distant hills. Galloway definitely scores on the scenic scale.

The long climb up Dunharberry Hill gave us a lenient leg-stretcher but once over the col, gradient went our way, we hung a sharp right, the track deteriorated and dropped for a short stretch of heaven-sent hammertime. It's a good thing the next junction was impossible to miss!

Beyond Barney Water Bridge we cruised down the Raiders Road to Stroan Loch. A chill pool set amid the flat, straw-coloured landscape of a winter marshland. The conical hump of Bennan Hill to the north begged for a recce so up we went. With each turn the trail degraded a little – raising our hopes for a technical, knuckle-jarring descent. Technical? A touch. But speed added spice for another pell-mell, wheel-to-wheel eliminator. This time with bonny views of Loch Ken spread out 450 ft below to tempt the eyes off the trail. But remember. This was mid-week, mid-winter so walkers were few. Few? There weren't any! In season this is a popular hike, so bikers beware!

Over Tannoch Flow we delighted in the sight of a track that dipped and dived into the forest. Galloway threw in a couple of twists and turns, the tyres stuttered but stuck to the rut and we slewed into the Raiders Road. Luckily dusk was well on the way – there were no tell-tale lights along this popular forest drive so we knew the road was clear all the way back to the car.

GLEN TROOL GRADIENTS
Distance: 27 miles. Climb total: 2600ft. Time: 3 hours.

Top out the forest's highest track, spin out the 4 mile descent to follow and get some air in those vents.

The 5 mile leg up to Bennan's summit would have been a breeze

Visit Galloway Forest in mid-winter and you'll have miles of trails to yourself

Start at Glen Trool Visitor Centre (GR372786). Exit L (ESE) from the car park on Loch Trool road for 0.25m then L (NE) onto 1st track into trees. 150yds then L (NW) at Y-junction, up for 1m to T-junction. On the return descent you'll go R here. Now keep SO (NNE) up main track for 1.5m then L (NNE) at T-junction for 2.5m climb onto Bennan.

Return 4m to go R (NW) at T-junction for 1.8m. L (WNW) for 1m (please use stile at forest edge) to Palgowan track. L (SW) 0.7m to road. L (S) for 0.25m then R (WNW) onto forest track. 0.4m then L (S) for 2m then L (E) at T-junction for 0.2m. Go R (SSW) by buildings to visit White Cairn. Otherwise SO (E) 0.2m to road.

R (S) on road 1.8m, past Glentrool village, to A714. L (SSW) 1m then 1st L (ENE) on lane 0.4m, over River Cree, to Minnigaff road T-junction. R (SE) 0.75m, over bridge, past car park and L (ENE) up forest track for 1.1m to T-junction. L (N) for 1.1m and keep L (N) at next T-junction for 2m descent to gate. Keep L through camp-site for 0.5m to Loch Trool road. L (SW) for 1.7m to start.

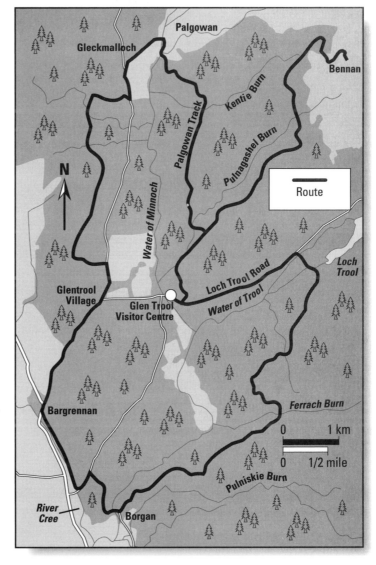

Palgowan

Gleckmalloch

Bennan

Kentie Burn

Palgowan Track

Pulnagashel Burn

N

Water of Minnoch

Route

Loch Trool

Loch Trool Road

Glentrool Village

Glen Trool Visitor Centre

Water of Trool

Ferrach Burn

0   1 km

0   1/2 mile

Bargrennan

River Cree

Borgan

Pulniskie Burn

but for the wind. At 500 ft below the top we quit the quiet of the trees for a stretch of windswept moor. The brisk breezes down in the glen had a big, big brother bellowing above. A bellow that had us fooled into thinking we had a Harrier jump-jet hovering overhead. Such was the force of the tempest barrelling down from the ridge, it whipped away front wheels and turned our measured progress into a wild and wayward zigzag dash for the next belt of trees.

Quiet. For a time. Cresting the final ridge and we slammed straight into the storm, stopped dead then got blown backwards! Biking was out. We couldn't even stand! So we sat on the track, backs to the wild wind with our legs over the bikes to stop them being blown away! But Nature wasn't going to pound us into submission. Composure recovered, we braced our weight against the frames and struggled to the summit, faces burning in the sub-zero

D I R E C T I O N S → → → → →

Start at the Clatteringshaws Forest Wildlife Centre (GR553766). On A712 go R (WSW). For Benninguinea leg take 1st track L (S) after 0.2m and follow red bike trail markers 2.2m to summit then return to road (watch those bends!). Continue (S) for 1m, over River Dee Bridge, then R (WNW) on Clatteringshaws ring road for 1m. L (SW) onto gated forest (Old Edinburgh) road for 1.8m. Track veers R, keep SO (SW) on deteriorating trail, crossing streams, for 1m down valley. L (S) for 100yds, over Black Loch Burn to forest track. R (W) to continue right round Black Loch, ignoring L turn at SW end, for 5m over Munwhul Hill to Craigencallie road. Go R (E) for 4.8m to A712

T-junction. L (N) for 200yds then R (SSE) into forest for 0.3m to fork R (S) onto Meikle Cullendoch track. Continue 6m, keeping L (SSE) at Grannoch Lodge T-junction and down by Big Water of Fleet River, to T-junction signed 'Loch Fleet'. Turn L (NNE) for 2.75m, passing Loch Fleet track on the L, to T-junction. Turn R (S) 0.8m down to T-junction then L (NNE) 1.2m, ignoring minor track off L, to next T-junction above Glengainoch valley. Keep R (NE) for 0.9m then keep L (NNE) on main track 1.6m, over Barney Water bridge, to T-junction. Turn R (SE) 1.6m to turn L (N) by Stroan Loch.

Climb 0.5m, ignoring R and L turns, then keep R (ENE) at

T-junction and on, over X-roads, 0.25m to T-junction on a bend. Go L (WNW) then almost immediately fork R (NW) for 1.2m, SO at 1st T-junction and alongside Bennan Hill, down to cross bridge. Turn R (N) for 1.6m, ignoring R turnings above Loch Ken, to T-junction. Turn L (SW) for 2.2m to Tannoch Flow, first up zigzag climb then R (WNW) at 1st T-junction, SO at next.

At Tannoch Flow T-junction go R (SW) to crest col for 1.5m descent to the Raiders Road and ignoring tracks off R. Go R (NW) for 5m, past Laggan o' Dee Farm, to A712. Turn R (NNE) to return 1m to start.

(-16°C in fact!) blast. Once there we weighted the wind-tossed Treks with rocks, sat in a crevice and had a cocoa stop. Even then it got blown out of my cup! Talk about whipped chocolate drinks!

Bikes braced against bodies we retraced our route along the ridge, ears deafened by the furore of the storm, fingers freeze-dried through the thickness of winter gloves. This was no place to picnic so, the instant we had the wind behind, we mounted up, took our chances with that tyrannical turbo-boost and flew down to the forest parrying side-swipe gusts on instinct alone. It worked. Increased speed added stability and we whizzed across that windswept moor, and into the forest with a slipstream roaring in our ears.

Time had slipped by on that manic mountain climb so we sped through shafts of sunlight and out of the plantation at Palgowan. From the road we got a fine view of Bennan, the Moors of Merrick

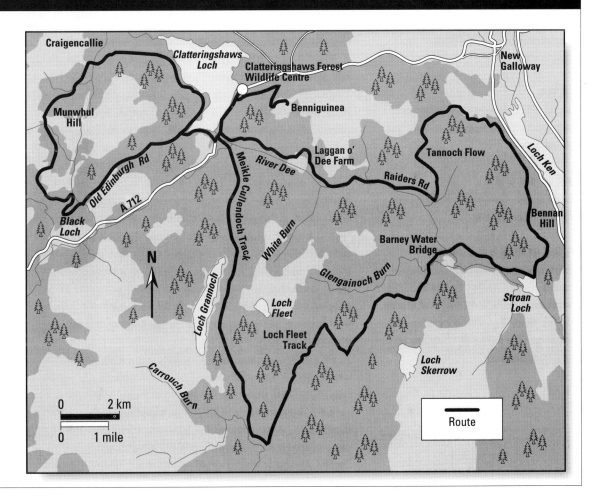

and the black clouds scudding above them. No wonder it was a polar-blasted hell up there! Golden sunlight cast long shadows, heralding an early sunset and Tim wanted a photo stop by the White Cairn above Glen Trool. Away we went, spinning down the long smooth cruise off Glencaird Hill. At the Cairn we perused the map, voted to add some extra evening mileage on the far side of Glen Trool below Larg Fell. It proved a real bonus. Expansive views and a twisty little downhill, through oak woods to the loch, all polished off by a wind-assisted homeward run.

GALLOWAY GRAND TOUR

Distance: 49 miles. Climb total: 4000ft. Time: 6 hours.

A touch of single track, some sweet chicanes and endurance is taken to extremes on a double loop by Clatteringshaws' shore.

Heavy snow. Muffled and white it had transformed Clatteringshaws Forest into an alpine wilderness. We'd hoped to complete the double loop before dark but, as the afternoon wore on, the snow got deeper and we cut it short, opting for a twilight tour of Craignell instead. A surrealist circuit it turned out to be.

Pale fire-road led us over the dark landscape below Brockloch Hill, tyres crunching a narrow trench through dry, powdery snow. Silence. Dusk and snow conspired to create an eerie hush; even the forest had ceased to listen. The fire-road dipped away and we struck out on the rough and ready Old Edinburgh Road. Creeping streams created an ice-cap that would have stretched the skills of Torvill and Dean – it face-planted me. More than once!

Entertaining and definitely a welcome change from top-cogging forest track, the Old Road single track terminated too soon at Black Loch. An apposite name reflected in the loch's obsidian surface. A popular venue in summer, the pristine snow round this dark pool showed no signs of passage today. We were definitely lone travellers. With dusk well advanced and a silent curtain of snow obliterating the braes we sensed more than saw the craggy shoulders of Craignell and Poultrybuie. Sporting just a 2.5-watt light between us I was anxious to get the long descent off Munwhul out of the way.

Puny lamps obscure more than they reveal so, *sans lumière*, we took off down the white ribbon that wound through the winter-scape. Our brief sojourn in the snow had taught us a thing or two: (1) ice + change in direction/speed = wipe-out; (2) ice + brakes = acceleration. Wipe-outs we'd already had, so acceleration was the name of the game. Ski terms – schuss, swing, hot-dogging – flashed through my mind as we hurtled down the hill, ruts and aggressively treaded rubber keeping it all together. Ethereal forms

INFO: CRIEFF

ACCESS

The nearest Scotrail (Tel: 01786 464754) station to Crieff is Gleneagles, 10 miles south. It is served by Sprinter trains so Inter-City travellers change at Edinburgh, Stirling or Perth (17 miles east of Crieff).

The M9 terminates at the Bridge of Allan. From there it's 18 miles to Crieff via the A85 and A822. Alternatively take the M90 north from Edinburgh to Perth and head west on the A85. The A85 and A822 also give access from the west and north respectively.

MAPS

OS 1:50 000 Landranger 52 Pitlochry to Crieff; OS 1:25 000 Pathfinders 335, 336, 348 and 349.

BIKE SHOPS

Wildcat Cycles (Tel: 01786 832321) in Bridge of Allan, Stirling.

ACCOMMODATION

There's everything from top-class hotels to camping. Crieff TIO (Tel: 01764 652578) has details. SYHAs at Stirling (Tel: 01786 473442), Perth (Tel: 01738 623658) and Glendevon (Tel: 01259 781206) are all about 18 miles away.

Beautiful Glen Turret behind and one lung-busting, granny-cog climb ahead (above)

A serpentine shooting track alongside Loch Turret takes you deep into the hills

of bikers danced through the snow and the Craigencallie road was reached without mishap.

Silence reigned supreme. But for the snow it would've been dark. As it was we could easily follow our pale pathway round the loch, though the odd dip and drift caught us out on occasion. The warm lights shining out from Craignell Cottage reminded us just how cold and dark it was. We hit the cranks and hummed down the ice-pack for home and a hot cuppa.

KETTLE CRUISE

Distance: 13 miles. Climb total: 1300ft. Time: 2 hours.

The perfect pre-amble to Highland trail-blazing with prime-time panoramas for company.

GLEN TURRET TOUR

Distance: 20 miles. Climb total: 3000ft. Time: 3 hours.

It's hard, it's fast and it's fun. Not for the timorous but ideal for the race trained.

We cruised west through Crieff to the Glen Turret distillery – well worth a recce and good for a wee dram – nestled in a verdant valley hard by the hamlet of Hosh. The day was bright and breezy, we were in ebullient spirits and just bursting to spin those cranks. Rubber hummed on tarmac as we spun through the lanes, sunlight flickered and spirits soared. So did the road. Not a calf-cruncher, but three miles of steady slog to kick city-bound calves into shape. Loch Turret Dam marked the end of tarmac and we hooked up on a tasty piece of track that hugs the shoreline on a roller-coaster run alongside the reservoir. A dun landscape broken by burns sparkling in the sunlight and, one that turned abruptly from a sheltered green glen into an austere and formidable range of fells. The bronze back of Ben Chonzie, the local Munroe and mountain

Once you're up all that pain pays dividends in the spectacular panoramas that unfold over Strath Earn

DIRECTIONS → → → → →   KETTLE CRUISE

Visit Glen Turret Distillery (GR858234) then follow lane (NW) 0.2m, turn L (N) for 3.3m – keeping R (ENE) on fork at 0.75m – up to building by dam. Cross stile onto track. This swings sharp R (E then S)) after which you follow main, contouring track with an occasional dip 'n' climb for 4.8m – keeping SO (NE) through junction at 1.8m – to T-junction 250yds before obvious cutting. Turn down R (SE) for 1.5m to A822 then R (SSW) 0.2m towards Crieff. Fork R (SW) onto track for 0.9m to lane at Monzie. Turn R (NW) and follow lane 2.4m back to Glen Turret Distillery. This route could be ridden counter-clockwise if there's an easterly wind.

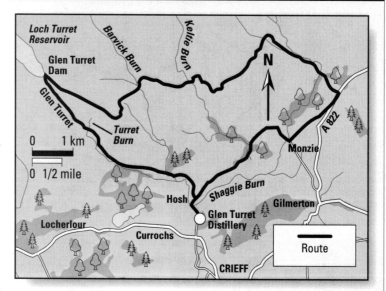

backdrop for much of the ride, still bore the remnants of a skirt of snow. Brilliant reminders of how severe the winter weather can be and how long it can hang on. Today was midsummer's eve; even so with each short climb the air added another nip!

But the short climbs on this track were just a jaunty forerunner. Your average Scottish byway doesn't doodle around in the depths of a glen for long and this one was no exception. A near sheer furrow, carved out of its precipitous flank held a track that climbed straight to the skyline. Surely not! An unrelenting mile of 1:4 climbing!

Up amongst the fell-tops views were beginning to unfold – just rewards for all that effort – but we had little time to appreciate the picturesque. Our track took a sudden dip and we dived round the steep shoulders of Ton Eich for a classic Highland fling that finaled in a lung-busting climb up onto Choinneachain Hill. Hemmed in by majestic mountains and heady Highland views, the sight of Strathearn's pastoral valley, sweeping away to the distant cerulean-blue Ochill Hills came as a scenic stunner!

Our destination was the distillery basking in the sun of that verdant valley bottom – 2200 ft of gravity suck on a tricky, twist-

Taking the Glen Turret roller-coaster to the hills

DIRECTIONS → → → → →　　GLEN TURRET TOUR

Visit Glen Turret distillery (GR858234) then follow lane (NW) 0.2m. Turn L (N) for 3.3m – keeping R (ENE) on fork at 0.75m – up to building by dam. Cross stile onto track. This swings R (E) and after 50yds turn L (NNW) alongside Loch Turret reservoir for 2.5m to T-junction. Turn R (SE) for big climb plus roller-coasters 2.25m – ignoring track off L (W) at 0.8m – to junction. Turn L (E) 100yds to Choinneachain cairn.

SO (E then SE) 3m – SO (E) at 0.25m and take care on loose section at 1.75m after chicane – to X-roads with CSWB sign. Turn L (NE) and follow obvious contouring track with an occasional dip 'n' climb for 3m to

T-junction 250yds before obvious cutting. Turn down R (SE) for 1.5m to A822 then R (SSW) 0.2m towards Crieff. Fork R (SW) onto

track for 0.9m to lane at Monzie. Turn R (NW) and follow lane 2.4m back to Glen Turret Distillery.

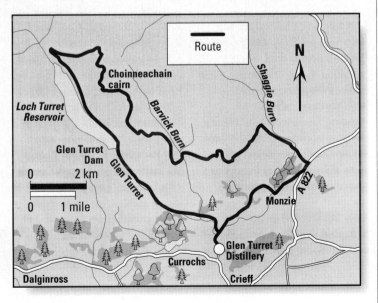

ing track that the map showed tumbling down contours, in a series of sensuous chicanes. We careered off the cairn-marked ridge and before long our tight little bunch had strung out into a serpentine line of speeding soloists. Each isolated in a private island of slip-stream roar, skipping skywards off bedrock ruts and slithering down precipitous slopes peppered with random rubble. A radical ride that had us seriously tempted to turn round for a rerun. But time was ticking onwards and we'd paid a big penalty for puncture repairs – keep the rubber rock hard unless you've got time and rims to spare.

Early evening sun flooded Strathearn in a golden chiaroscuro that threw the rolling pastureland into sharp relief. Even the mole-hills had shadows! We put in a fast cruise up above the valley, savouring the views except where short, sharp, dusty dips inter-rupted the scenic saunter and put our climbing skills to the test. All too soon we were dropping off the high road above the valley for a final dash to the valley bottom and a pell-mell road-race for home.

DIRECTIONS → → → → →

Visit Glen Turret distillery (GR858234) then turn R (NW then NE) and follow lane 2.4m to Monzie. Turn L (NE) up tarmac then dirt track for 0.9m to A822. Fork L (NNE) to T-junction with track, just after Newton Bridge, 5m away.

Turn L (NW) on track signposted 'Loch Tay' for 8.6m alongside River Almond to dam. We are requested by the landowners not to cycle off the track, to close gates and take care not to disturb livestock. Please also note that the shooting track that climbs (S) from the dam does not connect with our route 400yds (SW) of Dundornie, and is therefore not to be used.

Keep SO (WNW) on path alongside river for 1.2m, 150yds beyond island, then turn L (S) over

river and swing L (SE) on opposite bank downstream for 0.2m. Swing R (SSE) up intermittent path for 1.5m push/carry to low boggy col 400yds (SW) of Dundornie. Now keep L (E) of and above burn that runs (S).

From col keep SO (SSE) down gully, path becomes clear after 200yds then turns to track, for 2m to T-junction just after ford. Turn R (WSW) down track – with a sharp R (N) at 0.7m and a fork L (SE) at 1.3m – for 1.75m to gate at Coishavachan Farm. Go through then L (S) 225yds to lane, turn L (SE) for 4.25m to A85 in Comrie. SO (ESE) on A85 through Comrie – the Granary café is a good RR in village centre – for 1m to West Lodge camping site (a good start point if you're tenting it).

Go across entrance and SO (E) into forest via gate to T-junction 0.4m away. Turn L (N) 100yds up to T-junction then L (W) again for 0.5m – ignoring L (NW) branch at 0.3m – round L (N) hairpin, over stream to T-junction. Turn L (W then ENE) up zig-zag tarmac track – ignoring L (W) branches – 0.6m then keep R (E then N) on dirt track for 1m towards Braefordie Farmstead (deserted).

At fork keep L (NNW then NNE) for 0.7m to T-junction with main (NW/SE) track then turn R (SE) for 2.7m on roughly contouring route to Glen Turret Dam. Cross dam, turn R (S) on tarmac for 3.3m to T-junction with outbound route. Turn R (SW) and return 0.2m to Glen Turret Distillery.

GRAMPIAN DROVE

Distance: 38 miles. Climb total: 3500ft. Time: 6.5 hours.

Take the low road up the Glen and high-tail it down the high trail off the Ben.

The first leg's a long, steady run up Glen Almond on an old drove road with a rushing river for company. At Auchnafree we were waved down by a tweed-togged matron who took exception to our use of the track, relented and then gave us special dispensation to leg it up past Dundornie. Just this once. So don't you try it.

We had little choice about legging it. The old stalkers' track zigzagged but insufficiently for an in-saddle ascent all the way. At the head of the gully, with nowt more than an ovine-type indentation in the heather to follow, we shouldered the wheels and walked the quarter-mile to the col to rejoin the official route. Low cloud and drizzle turned on the dampers and we turned south for the big descent of the day.

Tyres squelched on some wet but welcome single track that took on a twin so we picked a rut apiece, put the hammer down and took on whatever the track dished out. Delights galore and, with gravity tugging hard on the tyres, some serious, spin-out speeds, plus one or two dented rims and burnt-out brakes by the time we hit the road in Glen Lednock. Oh, and let's not forget the scenery. It was spectacular!

The road down Glen Lednock to Comrie gave our buzzing legs time to relax before the sting in the tail that this ride had been waiting to deliver. A 1000ft climb to beat before we tasted the delights of the 3 mile descent from the Loch Turret Dam. Up through the forest the trail climbed in a series of calf-singeing

INFO: CRIEFF

RIGHTS OF WAY/ACCESS
In Scotland a 1984 Act and a 1930 Legal Ruling contradict each other by, on the one hand, specifically outlawing cycling without consent along footpaths and, on the other, specifically stating that you can cycle along a right of way. Add to that the fact that trespassers can only be prosecuted if it can been proven that they have caused damage, and you have a recipe for freedom to roam for all. In practice this isn't so, though landowners – like the Glen Turret Estate – are tolerant of considerate cyclists. So keep to paths and tracks, walk when there's any doubt and, if you're not on a right of way, leave if the owner asks you to. Our trio of trails are not all on rights of way.

The Glen Turret, Glen Almond and Glen Lednock hills depend on grouse and deer stalking for their revenues. There are seasonal restrictions on access; mid-August to mid-October is generally the most sensitive time. Any individual seeking access to these areas is advised to obtain permission first from the relevant estate offices.

For information on rights of way in Scotland contact the Scottish Rights of Way Society, 10/2 Sunnyside, Edinburgh EH7 5QA.

switchbacks, quadriceps quivered and granny cogs spun ever so slowly, as a severe thirst burned my throat with every foot climbed. We took a brief RR up by Braefordie Farm. With the last big climb behind us and the beauties of Strathearn once more below us, we were tired but by no means beat. Mind you, if I'd doused my sizzling calves in the water butt it would have boiled!

The panoramas this side of Strathearn were even more picturesque than those from the far side of Loch Turret, and our return to tarmac by the Turret dam was definitely tinged with regret. All too soon we'd creamed down to the distillery and the day's ride was done.

Cooling hot blocks off in Barvick Burn above Crieff

The rugged terrain of Galloway's Glenkens has been opened up by commercial forestry, and is ideal mountain biking country

Appendices

THE CYCLISTS TOURING CLUB

Since 1878 the Cyclists Touring Club (CTC) has been the governing body for recreational cycling in this country. It is recognised by organisations such as the Sports Council, the Department of Transport and the Department of the Environment. Membership is open to anyone interested in cycling. They currently have 40,000 members, 200 nationwide clubs and 100 local clubs affiliated to them.

Recently the CTC has taken on responsibility for addressing off-road cycling access issues, which include promoting rights of way initiatives wherever they occur and representing the views of mountain bikers at local and national levels. Local representation is done through a network of volunteer access officers. Please remember that they are volunteers and carry out their CTC duties without payment and in addition to their normal employment, so please contact them only if there is genuine need.

If you would like to apply for membership then please contact:

CTC, Dept CSB/94, 69 Meadrow, Godalming, Surrey GU7 3HS.
Tel: 01483 417217.

Benefits of being a member include:
    Representation on rights of way and access issues in your area.
    Third party insurance cover.
    Free legal advice for cycling-related problems.
    Free legal aid.
    Free technical advice.
    Free international touring info.
    Bi-monthly colour magazine.
    Free handbook.
    Mail order service.
    A voice in the world of MTBing.

Route index

Author's Acknowledgements

My personal and heartfelt thanks to –

the many 'local' riders who helped compile the routes first published in *MTB Pro* 'Pro-Trails' – you know who you are. There are thousands of beaming bikers out there who are indebted to your efforts and generosity;

The rights of way folk in the relevant counties and National Parks, the various water companies and the Forest Enterprise.

For technical support and back-up: Ralph Coleman Cycles, Taunton, Somerset; Madison; Shocktech; Michelin Tyres.

For loan of hardware: Timax Ti MTB frames; Shocktech forks; Halson forks; Middleburn drive systems; IBC hydraulic brakes; USE seat-pins; Avocet computers.

For loan of software: Polaris MTB clothing; North Wave MTB boots; Giro helmets; Buffalo outdoor clothing; Sub-Zero thermals.

The enthusiastic MTBers I've had the pleasure of sharing a trail with, many of whom appear in the photographs used to illustrate this book. Likewise – you know who you are.

Tym Manley. (It's all his fault. Honest!)